Day of the Dog

Day of the Dog

Douglas K. Pearson

Day of the Dog
© 2008 Douglas K. Pearson
Storymakers, LLC

All rights reserved.

Edited by David Egner
Cover design by AUXILIARY Advertising & Design
Book design and layout: Dave Gilman

Printed in the United States of America
11 12 13 /CS/ 10 9 8 7 6 5 4 3 2 1

Acknowledgements

A serious thank you goes to Tim Williams, a retired Police Detective, who had a part in the arrest and conviction of one of Grand Rapids' most horrible serial rapists. I also thank him for giving me countless hours as he helped correct the police procedure stuff in this novel that I just made up when I wrote it.

A special appreciation goes to Robert Lucas, a master teacher and youth worker who I first met at Island Christian School in the Florida Keys. I once kept him awake all night by this story that came alive as we drove a busload of teens back to the Keys from a D.C rally.

A galactic thanks of sincere appreciation to my life-long counselor, mentor and my late-father's best friend, David C. Egner, who believed in my writing so much, he rejected my first 14 novels. I thank him for the day when he told me that my latest round of stories didn't stink; the day he re-dipped his red pen and came out of retirement to make them readable. The day he showed me that a father's life cut short, lives on in the hearts of friends.

And I give the deepest, all-heart gratitude to two other Florida Key residents. Father Gerry of San Pablo Catholic Church in Marathon Key and John Sutter of Key Largo. They are the Nephelim of Genesis 6 to me. They are heroes of old, men of renown.

No animals were injured in the writing of this book.

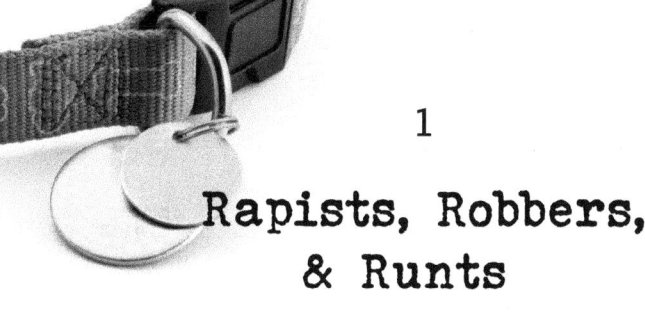

1
Rapists, Robbers, & Runts

Shy Wendell Shyly paused on the edge of the dark, vast field and readied himself to counter-attack and rescue Deontra Schnidorf from some dirt bag, punk thugs. Night had fallen an hour ago, but still he waited, watching some sapling pine trees take the shape of black pirate sails on a midnight sea. A breeze even blew waves across the long grasses around them. Beyond these shadows, a drone of a car hummed by, its lights beaming across an asphalt road.

Wendell eyes were well adjusted to the tar-like air, but still couldn't see much. Beyond the road, he saw the faint glow of friday night football lights reflecting off some low clouds above Tremble High School.

He was a sophomore there.

After another long pause, he stepped away from the tangled woods of toadstool covered fallen trees. With a final glance back at the gurgling river, he left the thick foliage that was upstream from the town of Tremble.

Despite the cool night breeze, sweat slimed inside his non-latex gloves. Gray clouds oozed under a black, star sprinkled sky and a football game crowd roar drifted down to him.

Wendell inhaled deep, trying to slow his heart which had now colored his pale face with blood stress. He ghosted deeper into the waist high grasses undetected. Upon seeing the cut of the faint trail in the swaying weeds, he merged into one of the pine trees and recalled what he had overheard in lunch line yesterday.

"She'll be there!" the voice had said in a gut tone.

"How do you know?"

"She Convents every Friday! Bam Bam said so. She hates her!"

"You really wanna nail Deontra near a convent? You sure? Holy Ground? Holy crap!"

"Bam's got some serious hate going," another had said. "What's in it for us?"

At this they had laughed. A ghoulish growl. The type of grunts that gave melody to dirty dirges sung in stale basements.

Shyly's ears had perked at the sound of Deontra's name as he eavesdropped. When Wendell had first seen Deontra Schnidorf a year before, he had an out-of-body experience.

She had aligned his planets.

The click of Deontra's heals in that empty hallway was the stuff that inspired symphonies.

Him seeing her walk had started a never-ending concert in his head and he only had to close his eyes to see her dark hair dance down her back!

Now Shyly's left hand grasped his flat black, re-curve hunting bow. He didn't like this place. *And I hate them! And all people to a point. And talking! Why do I have to talk? Even better, why do I have to hear myself talk? I bother me! Frick'n Loser!*

Five Broad Head, razor-tipped arrows were clipped to his bow frame. *They will talk for me tonight!*

The bow had come from his uncle years ago. His Uncle Jon had said, "Keep it! I won't tell your parents if you don't!" Uncle Jon liked secrets. He liked passivity. He knew who he was. He was a true Shyly.

It had taken Wendell hours to sterilize the arrows of finger prints and DNA. He knew he wouldn't get all the dogs on this night. It would take some time and he needed to slow down the cops as much as possible.

All those who planned to assault Deontra would pay more than piper wages!

"You dare touch her, you dare to die!" Wendell whispered, his breath releasing white vapor against the night like a dragon would. "So Mutt the Mongrel is loose! And now your sniffing Deontra," he hissed.

Not many knew Mutt's real name.

Wendell did.

Mutt's name was Sid Mongrel.

Students and most of the teachers called Sid, Mutt. They did this because Mutt was scumbait.

Mutt was the alpha dog in the wolf pack he called his friends. He was farm boy big but his frame didn't carry an athletic build, it carried a man build. He had man strength from farm work that had started him off most mornings around 4am. He must have been the pick of the litter for his old man.

Mutt wanted his dogs to be seen as a gang, but nobody cared about the slobbering foursome. Banished from the mainstream, they have been hounding the borderlands and shadows of the school turf.

"I'm hunting dogs!" Wendell repeated under his breath. He would shoot the closest dog and scatter the pack with the power of rescue. Then he would yank his razor-tipped, Broad Head arrow from the carcass and float downstream to a canoe ramp and retreat home, scentless and trackless. It would be a clean kill. The first of however many showed up.

Football lights turned some dark clouds to grey in the east.

Wendell's mop of blond hair, stuffed under a black hat, started heating up. He wiped sweat off his forehead with a sleeve and eyed the dark field linking the convent to school property. *What kind of Catholic stuff do you do there, Deontra?* Wendell thought as he saw a nun through a window, then his eyes caught shadows darting across the dark pathway from school.

One dog took to weeds; another went behind a small tree.

The attack was real!

It was coming!

Wendell tried to swallow, but his stomach fluids became like mercury. He wondered for the first time if he could scare off predators hungry enough to go after a girl like Deontra.

Deontra was a Catholic girl. A good Catholic girl.

Knuckles groaned as Wendell's left hand clamped the bow and he tried to blink away his fear. His guts churned and tightened. He notched an arrow.

Deontra appeared on the path to his far left. Her thick black hair was darker than night itself. All else, treelines and tall grasses, paled to shades of gray compared to her black hair. It flowed in the breeze like the stuff of legends.

Wind rustled leaves. Riverbank mud bit into Wendell's nose as he strained. Even in the dark, his mind knew enough detail of her body, hair and perfume to fill in the missing pieces. He noticed the difference between the convent to his right and the darkness of the barren field before him where the stalkers hid.

He smiled. He was ready to do what must be done. He was ready to rescue.

Deontra walked toward the trap.

"Keep moving!" Wendell whispered as his three right fingers stretched bowline back to his cheek, bending the recurve 35 lb. Bear™ hunting bow. He looked down the arrow and exhaled completely to prepare for the full breath that would power his yell.

The attack struck Deontra from behind in a dull, hard take-down, knocking her forward. Her schoolbooks flew out in front of her, their pages fluttering like white doves against a black curtain.

Then shadows near Wendell pounced on Deontra.

All was still.

No explosive scream.

Her muffled gasps of fear and horror got slapped quiet by what sounded like rubbery wings of a large bat.

All was wrong.

Horror continued.

High on the high school bleachers, where football scouts perch, take notes and roll videotape, Jones Watson sat with four friends. They were doing some note taking of their own. They didn't like the proximity of video cameras because they had to guard what they said.

Last summer Watson's crooked cronies netted $19,000. But now with Ace Dingle, the California Kid, they were broadening the reach of their sticky little fingers. Tonight they planned to add more jingle to their jangle.

They figured 2,000 Tremblens stacked the bleachers to watch Ron Robertson, the first legitimate D-1 QB in school history.

Being a head taller than most on the field and an arm like an RPG, Ron was easy to spot.

Michigan University was scouting him tonight; the big fella from that program spent most of the time on his cell phone.

Watson smiled at the crowd. His thick black hair matched his leather coat and they both kept him warm against the sharp autumn breeze that was whirling at the bleacher tops. He had arranged for the visitors to buy tickets in Tremble at the last minute because Watson had flooded the opponent's school with identical ticket rolls so more cash would come to

Tremble.

As predicted, someone, probably Athletic Directors, worked out a plan and set up a separate gate so the money split would be fair. The bogus tickets were another lead police would follow, and like the others, it would have them chasing their little curly tails.

Adults paid $5, students $3, and after the game the same old Booster Lady, Maybell King, took the football gate money and concession earnings to the night depository at Tremble State Bank, just as she had done in the rotten years when it was pocket change.

Maybell King was over seventy years old, kept a wade of long silver hair balled up behind her head in a bun. She had rich blue eyes. Young eyes. And they were in sharp contrast with her tired, sagging facial skin. She had poured her salt and sugar into providing the best popcorn, hotdogs, candy and coffee for Tremble football fans for many a decade. Her four sons had all captained their teams back in the day and had spread fear and trembling to many a opposing team. They moved on but Maybell never outgrew her Booster role to the Tremble High School Football Program.

Maybell King had been collecting, counting and depositing Tremble High football proceeds since Jesus converted the short little greedy guy!

Maybell owned six cats and fed a dozen strays.

Watson knew all this but it was Ace who helped him imagine the possibilities! And because of the California Kid, Watson figured there was ten, maybe eleven grand all in the hands of old, cat-loving, Maybell King!

Wendell Shyly fell to his knees, stunned. His mind swirled like a fish hit by a boat propeller.

The muffled gasps for air seemed harmless until the tear of Deontra's clothing ripped through the night and silenced crickets.

Wendell tried to step but his spine became like Jell-O cubes stuck together with toothpicks. Not yet able to inhale, his opened mouth gaped as if the planet's air was gone. The tension on the bowline exhausted his arm and it withdrew harmlessly as his pants wetted with urine. He weakened as they bored down on her and his mind filled with broken glass. Wendell unleashed the arrow at the convent, but it disappeared as if shot off a cliff.

Shivering, he dropped his hands into the dirt and his fingers landed on a stone. It was round and just larger than a quarter. From his knees, he hurled it at the convent. It clanged off a window, having neither velocity or mass to break glass.

The noise did make two attackers stand vertical like prairie dogs.

And a head did appear in that second floor window.

But none of this did Wendell see, for his eyes had filled with sting.

Then floodlights killed the darkness and the convent yard went green with life.

"Talk of this and I'll eat your bones!" Mutt barked to the crumpled girl, then he and his dogs scampered off.

"Who's there? Deontra?" a nun asked from the far off doorway.

Wendell stood to replay. He then saw her and froze like deadwood in winter.

Deontra appeared to have fallen down a rocky mountain. Her body was twisted wrong. She gasped, sound not making it past Wendell.

A nun entered the yard, taking a few feeble steps into dew

tipped grass. "Deontra?"

Deontra twisted and came about to her knees. Out of the weeds, clothes askew, her voice cried out. "Over here!"

Wendell watched her try to stand, falter down then get on her legs. Any breeze could topple her. Her hair was full of leaves, grass and twig. Dirt and blood was on her arms and face. She lifted a hand and a finger was bent wrong. Her face winced wrinkles as she tried to clench a fist despite the dislocation.

Stomach acid surged into Wendell's mouth and gagged him, burning rot into his taste buds. His nose was steamed raw and he could smell himself as the ground rose up to press against his face.

Then the Nun saw horror. She screamed and rushed to the edge of the floodlights that now illuminated the disorientated Deontra.

Deontra fell into the woman's arms and they limped from the edge of the field onto the mowed grass of the convent's yard and there they collapsed.

Other nuns, summoned by the call, converged on Deontra. The team lifted Deontra and ushered her into the convent.

One lone nun, a very old one, lingered under the light and stared into the darkness of the field, her right arm made a sign of the cross as if to ward off monsters. She kept doing it as she backed across the yard and into sanctuary.

Wendell watched this nun from his knees, and heard her lock the door as his vomit erupted. He gagged, sobbed and fell on pine needles. Phlegm dangled from his chin as sand-covered fingers tried to rub clean his eyes.

Shame crushed him into the ground.

No ambulances or police came for Deontra.

Now at the edge of nun property, at the very spot where

one of the Sisters faced when she signed the cross, memory slapped Wendell as if *he* were the monster. He balanced on his knees. *Why not? Why can't I?* His hand went to his mouth and touched teeth. It seemed his eyeteeth *were* growing.

A strong crowd roar followed a big play from the football game and stirred Wendell back to real time.

He smelled his stink, drew a leg under himself, stood and walked to where Deontra had lost her books. Bending down, he stacked them neatly. He was dazed. He had failed Deontra. Rubbing his teeth again, he turned in a full circle.

He will never fail her again.

2
Broken & Borderlines

Army surgeon John Carp had been Dishonorably Discharged from the Vietnam Conflict for killing wounded soldiers. In all fairness to the doctor, the army men had been severely wounded, were almost dead and nearly insane with pain. Carp never killed just anyone, and had seen his acts as merciful. Dr. Carp had standards. Either way, it didn't go over well with Armed Forces Medical Policy to have a military doctor pillow talk dying soldiers. But since the press was ugly on the war to begin with, Uncle Sugar just booted Dr. Carp out of Saigon.

By 1972 Carp's gaunt, rawboned 6'5" frame had landed in the quiet farming community of Tremble, Michigan, and he was soon eyeing the town's sick animals from underneath his military crewcut. Standing outside the city limits is when he had first heard the whisper of purpose, so he went back to school and earned his veterinarian license. It took two years. Human and animal anatomies were more different than he thought. But book smarts and licenses had never warmed the vet's cold eyes that peered out from behind strong walls of bone that jutted out from his skull. Nor had education given him social graces.

So when Tremblens talked about their Vietnam Veterinarian, they did so quietly. It seemed his huge, President Mondale ears could detect the slightest whisper.

"I Keep Them Walking Cheap" reads his mailbox sign, which is not *entirely* true, since he had saved an inbred Rottwieller pup with severe hip displacement. The dog was begging for the body bag until Carp amputated the little hind legs and rigged a pink tricycle tire under its stomach so its big front paws could wheel itself around.

In return the dog, now named Agent Orange, works for Dr. Carp as a bouncer of sorts. He's named after the Vietnam brush and brain killing chemical, Agent Orange. The dog controls the routines of all animals in Carp's Clinic, herding cats to top selves and limiting tomfoolery. Only when Agent Orange sleeps or gets stuck in a rut do the cats launch hunger insertions to the kitchen where bowls of food are scattered across the floor and where the sign on the door to the bathroom reads, TOILET WATER TASTE BETTER.

Carp's kitchen is the Land of Milk and Honey for the recovering and down-and-out pets of Tremble. The one's who were born into families who couldn't afford to go to the clean, good-health-pet-spa-of-proper-boundaries, on the other side of Tremble's DMZ.

But despite Carp's tough talk and image, the whole town knows he is better than most in identifying with Tremble's wounded, ailing and expendable pets.

City leaders had given him the deer and varmint roadkill contract decades ago, and Carp had been scraping up whatever had gotten creamed on Tremble's by-ways ever since.

Cops and DOT call in dead deer locations to Carp all the time.

Insurance companies love Carp too, because his renowned tracking ability has reduced car-deer crash fraud.

And once word had gotten out that Carp dealt with the dead, folks across the whole county started carting off their aged and used up pets to Carp because he doesn't charge a nickel to put an animal down.

Four years ago a boy had limped into Dr. Carp's obscure

pet clinic with a broom handle rammed through the meaty part his calf. The knock on the door had been a flat, open palmed, haunting slap.

Carp, wearing a de-sleeved combat shirt, had used one of his long, vein-lined arms to open the door to a City Police officer.

"I'm Officer Weary and this here's my nephew." The puddle glum officer said, nodding down to an adolescenting boy of zits and crewcut hair.

"I thought you was fired," Carp said to the man as he looked at the crude spear stuck in the boy's leg.

"Tomorrow's my last day," the cop had said. He tried to smile at this but the black sacks under his eyes seemed to cement a scowl on his face.

"And this here's your pet?" he asked as some sleeping, back-row memories stirred Carp's mind as the kid's face grimaced. *Figures. So the kid's mom was a Weary that married into the Spamp family.* Carp knew. Officer Weary and now Spam were the last of the bloodline to a family that had given Tremble an aftertaste of sheer unpleasantness. Spamp family history, however short, was a train wreck of pain.

"Whatever it takes. I'm done with this here town and I'm done overseeing my sister's kid. Oh. Forgot. He doesn't talk. He'll sometimes look at you when you call him, Spam."

"Why me?"

"Who else? You're the only one who deals with the dead." Officer turned, creaking his Kevlar and opened the door to his Oldsmobile Cutlass.

"Where's your cruiser?" Carp called out. He couldn't resist.

"Good bye, Carp. Bye Spam," the officer had said and drove off, his car nearly dragging it butt on the road. *Fitting. Some men can't hack being cops.*

Carp grunted approval. He liked men who moved on and

he kind of favored people who made others sick. The doctor poked his head outside, looked around, then waved Spam inside with a big cotton swab gummed thick with brown paste that he had just scooped from a German shepherd's infected ear.

"So you don't talk, huh?" Carp had said.

The boy had squared his shoulders and mustered a breath. "I haven't spoke in over three years." He said from a pie face with little ears and a crocked nose that had healed wrong after a break. His eyes were as defeated and small as they come.

"So much for that. You just spoke to me. You got a name?"

"I decided to speak to you."

"That's beautiful. What's your name?" Carp had rubbed whiskers that felt like ends of metal paper clips. "Why're you here? Are you really the Spam Kid?"

"You and I are going to be friends. I am Josh Spamp," he said as he limped by the man and towards the stainless operating table.

"Ahhh! So you *are* one who burned up your brother!"

Spam looked at his feet.

"Well, I smelled enough Nam-napalmed Charlies to feel bad for you. It true you lit the match that made him go ca-flewy?" Carp followed him in. "I ain't likable, Spam. My only friend is Agent Orange. I just scalpel the Village Critters for money."

The boy had made it to the stainless steel operating table, blood squeaking in his sneaker. He managed to get on top.

"Then treat me like a dog, Dr. Carp. Treat me like the dog I am!" Spam dropped to his back and held out his speared leg.

"Then beat it, you bloody mutt!" he reached down and yanked out the stick, which now appeared to have been sheared off from a broom or yard rack handle.

Spam burped out a short, wincing scream, but smothered it.

"And take your bloody stick with you!" he held out the spear.

Spam sat back up then. "But you and I are to be friends."

Not bad with the pain, Carp thought. But it had offended Dr. Carp, nevertheless. "Friends huh? You mean it? You'd stick this nasty swab in your ear to prove it?"

Spam had taken the mucusy swab and plunged it in his ear. The vile wax stuck.

"It can't be!" Carp had gagged the words and dropped the stick.

Nearby dogs had salivated as they chased after the blood-dipped stick. But it was double treat night and they soon tore into Spam's bloody shoe that was on the floor. Agent Orange snatched that snack and rolled away, the pack of dogs tailgating after him.

Now the boy called Spam is 16 and that particular illegal broomstick surgery had happened four years ago.

It was a Friday night and Spam was late.

Carp paced.

Agent Orange wheeled.

Carp looked at the same long swab that had come from the dog's ear and went into Spam's. It was now nearly black and taped to his mirror. It was a good memory. It had started the best friendship the man had ever had. The memory was the only good thing about that mirror. It kept growing deeper grooves into the man's face and longer rogue hairs on his eyebrows.

Carp's long legs gambled him into the room where he froze roadkill. He reached into the cupboard above the freezers and his long, swollen-knuckled fingers pulled out a .45 automatic, the same weapon that had been his companion since war days in Saigon. He shoved it inside his belt and walked back into his clinic.

He knew why he was nervous.

Some secrets weigh heavy on a man.

Spam would arrive any minute and then Carp would have to decide.

It was time to tell Spam.

3
Skirts & Coats

Pamela Stanford, cheerleader El Capitan, danced, twirled and bounced for quarterback Ron Robertson. Her fine, thin blond hair swirled continually. After tonight's game they were to celebrate the one month anniversary of their first kiss. She always had felt her lips were too thin, but behold, the power of makeup! She flashed a smile at her squad. Her hard work and investments promised high payoff!

Her team beamed a back-at-ya smile as if their faces were little mirrors. The seven sisters of her school spirit squad chirped and chimed how Ron, the catch of the school, had been hooked by one of theirs! It made them all feel more beautiful.

But Pamela's heart was heavy despite her high-flying jumps. She was hurt. *How could she be Ron's second choice after Deontra?*

Pamela knew Catholic virtue was an oxymoron so she had launched her simple plan and had followed Sid Mongrel to Ample's Gas Station yesterday. She had bought his brand of cigarettes.

He had smiled as two of his thick fingers took the pack as they rounded the corner and sat by his fire hydrant. "How's the stuff, Pamela?"

"What do you think? It's good. Your stuff is always good!" She had thanked him by taking a drag on his smoke.

"Always will be! Need more?"

"Of course! *And* I got a free one for you too," she had said.

That got Mutt thinking. Long ago, before Pamela had upgraded her social standing, they had secretly shared more than spit.

She knew he still had lust for her and she envied how he could live in a world of anarchy. As she explained, and got him tracking on her idea, he didn't ask questions. Then she left him.

Mutt had stayed on, sniffing her lipstick on the cigarette butt and drooling over her plan. Then he snuffed his smoke out on the iron dumping cap where semi-trucks accessed the buried 80,000 gallon fuel tanks.

Now the crowd roared Pamela back to Ron and the football game. She was back in her flawless uniform of red and white, color-coded in public with her quarterback.

She watched her Ron get bounced around by comrades covered in grass stains, slapping each other in celebration.

His stare fixated on her and she beamed and swirled her skirt up for him. It was the least she could do at that distance.

Their eyes then broke off as Ron got hoisted onto the shoulders of his teammates. Only then did Pamela hold still and look beyond the ticket gate, over the barbed wire stadium fencing, across the parking lot and down the hill. Her mind left the floodlights and footballs and entered the field by the convent. The right side of her mouth turned up. Her eyes went back to Ron. *You're all mine now, Ron. You're all mine now!*

At the edge of Tremble's industrial section where most small businesses had failed, Spam lumbered up the sagging steps of Carp's Clinic and pushed open the door, rattling the rusty can of .45 cartridges below the interchangeable number sign that read, '6' DAYS SINCE LAST EUTHANASIA.

Tremblens logically assumed Carp was still suffering from the war. After all, children got a .45 brass bullet casing with each visit and the gun powder smell was always fresh. Plus they knew the rumors. So no one noticed that the sign appeared when Carp had acquired 720 acres east of town from Widow Thompson in 1976. But because Thompson land was bog land, and since the Department of Natural Resources held dominion over swamps, it was as worthless as the sinking barns the Thompsons had raised a century ago. Either way, no one gave much attention to the ways of Carp.

But for Carp the land was the bombshell gift of a lifetime. It gave him purpose.

Spam noticed a dozen bullet shells in the can. He smiled. He felt good. His scoliosis wasn't nagging him because his backpack was empty after four years of lugging books. He recalled the stupid question he had asked long ago.

"What's those?" Spam said, pointing to a bookshelf while the vet showed him how to field-dress his stabbed leg.

"So you're a stupid mute?" Carp had asked.

"Probably."

"They're books."

"What's in em?"

"Read them! Then go to the library and get ten more."

That's how Spam, at age twelve, had learned to read. He became the only member of Dr. Carp's Reading Club. Being a bright boy, he eventually became brilliant. Having only a life of social pain outside the clinic, he sometimes devoured three books a day, as he sat in one of Carp's non-dog recliners, sipping Mountain Dew as his long-fingernails scratched scum from his scalp. During the last 1500 days, Spam had read much of Tremble's library and covered his chair, several times oven in dead skin. As Spam had sat in the clinic and read, Carp busied himself, poking, prodding and cutting many a pet, handling county road kill and the growing flow of aging and unwanted pets.

Somewhere along the line, Carp added a few chest freezers to better store dead deer until Disposal Day. Friday was when he needed help lugging frozen venison from the freezers into his truck, and corralling, caging and loading animals that had been handed their dismal Black Spot by their very owners. Out of love no doubt.

With no books, Spam now glided up into the animal clinic. Dr. Carp came from around the corner wiping his hands with a towel.

"I'm finished reading your book list!" Spam said.

"Umm! Carp said. "Well, Happy Birthday! I got a surprise for you!" He tapped the worn holster on his hip holding his Vietnam .45.

Now Spam had seen Carp strap on that gun every Friday for years. Spam walked to the three chest freezers and opened their lids and noticed only a few deer.

"What happened this week?" Spam asked. "Only three?"

"I can't figure it out. It must be the heat." Carp seemed concerned for some reason.

Spam took front hooves, Carp grabbed back ones and they slung the mangled roadkill deer into Carp's truck bed. Then they loaded up the cages of tired, aged pets that had been dropped off during the week.

Carp always handled the dead on Fridays and Spam long since knew it was Carp's favorite day. Friday night euthanasia was Carp's passion. Caged animals went primal. Even ones with three paws in the ground heard the whisper of instinct and pitched a howling stink.

"We got a good bunch of frantic varmints tonight!" Carp said.

"We?" Spam questioned, wheezing in his lungs from loading the deer carcasses and cages. "There ain't no 'we' in what you do on Friday nights, Carp."

"Hey. Tonight I got a surprise for you," Carp said.

"I'll bet."

"I want you to come with me!"

Spam looked at the man's .45. "I don't know, Carp."

"What?"

"What? You know. The cages always come back empty. And you always oil your gun."

"It's time you come, Spam. Trust me," he patted the gun again. "You'll like it."

"No. I've seen enough death to last a life time."

"Suit yourself," Carp said. "But it ain't as bad as it looks."

"Ya. Right," Spam said and retreated inside and took up a Carp book. In an hour or so Carp would return and go straight to the table to clean off gunpowder residue and oil his pistol.

4
Holy Rollers & Highwaymen

An hour after the final trumpet sounded, ending the Friday night football game, Angie Stone, the small in stature but large in heart leader of Tremble Baptist Youth (TBY), divvied out paintball guns to seven teenagers at Reveered's house. Time for Holy War. It was TBY's AGA or After Game Activity.

Reveered hosted. He was a young man out of Bible college, maybe twenty-four years old, who was thinking about becoming a real pastor. He and his wife were married but one year and their house was north of town on the southern edge of farm country and woods. They had some acreage split by a creek.

His wife usually left and did something out-of-town in the big city when teenagers arrived. "You mixing guns and church may be American, but that doesn't make it right!" she said whenever the opportunity came. It was a growing concern because her husband seemed to be more like a killer than a healer at AGA.

He made new ambush spots on his property every week.

AGA Holy War was simple. Two teams. Heathens and Martyrs. Girls against boys. Angie led her Heathens (for pretend of course) who had to respect and tolerate all *but* the intolerable. They could shoot the intolerable. They got semi-automatic paintball guns and tons of ammo. Their bullets whizzed about 300 feet per second.

A boy named Luke, a bushy red-haired teenager, captained the Martyrs, the one's who listened to God's Higher

Calling, followed the beat of The Big Drummer Boy, and violated Heathen-Law-of-Mutual-Respect both in theory and practice.

Hence Holy War.

Reveered had long ago made a deck of theology cards so all knew who they ought to be.

Players got anxiety from Wild Cards. Untamed cards were dangerous and could convict a Heathen to be a Martyr or seduce a Christian to betray his fellowship. They brought paranoia to Heathens and teased Martyr's with despair. Cards could change a game. If you were a Heathen and got the wrong card you had to run for your life or you could be shot on sight. If you were on the Martyr side, a wild card could get you tied up with the chosen Martyr. Or banished, only to be hunted down and shot by the other team.

Cards stated the obvious, like how Martyr's kneel to God alone and how Heathens hate absolutes. But they also caused grudges, which carried over from week to week. Luke and Angie were currently in feud. But in general, the two teams knew their fates. One had to die, the other had to kill.

Reveered readied the cards. Games went quick. Each boy got publicly martyred once a week under the tree at Execution Stand. Fair's fair.

Players now circled Reveered.

"When will tomorrow come? When will the tolerant kill the intolerant?" Reveered asked from behind a face of black and green grease paint. When he held still on any given night, he was all but invisible with his military grade, Boreal Forest camouflage gear.

Four boys looked at their only pitiful paintball gun, a first generation pump-action Black Talon with four paintballs.

"I'm adding and extra thought spark tonight to get the fire going," Reveered said. "Listen to this. When will violence, which our country preaches as gospel, begin to reap God's wrath for butchering his creation?"

The seven teenagers looked at each other. All was quiet except the night birds calling up from the forest. Luke shook his head. It was a trick question.

"Just a thought," Reveered said. "Let's start!" He turned to the boys. "Martyrs?"

"We will love our enemies to our deaths!" the boys chanted in unison.

"Heathens?" Reveered turned to the girls.

"We will tolerate all but the intolerant! They must be executed without remorse!" The girls chanted in unison.

Reveered dealt the cards.

Players drew cards to their chests and drifted off to their teams.

Reveered then took up *his* paintball gun. It fired 14 balls a second. That's why they called him, Reveered. His role in Holy War was the constant; he played the Anti-Christ. The mobile henchman who stacked the deck. He marched past the girls.

"You.. . . . You're not going to be with us?" Angie's delicate fingers went to last week's paintball bruise. Luke's gift. It shook as she lit the candles on Stone Table where they baited the Christian with a Bible.

"Just keep them frightened and you'll win."

"Where are you going? You'll help us, right?"

"I have a baptism to undergo." Reveered said from behind black and green Marine Corp paint and girls watched him step into the night.

Backs against candles, guns aimed outward, the three girls locked and loaded. No Martyr was going to get past them to Stone Table if they could help it. No Martyr was going to get their hands on the Bible tonight!

Once alone, Reveered immersed himself into creek water, blended in with a log and waited for war to begin. The icy, spring-fed current was like thorns in his skin until his right side numbed. He would have to shoot left handed. That was okay. Sheople always come to the shepherd.

Off to the other end of Reveered's property line, boys of Resistance felt the heat. They grouped after darting off from the others and were now on top of the hill under the big tree at the edge of the forest. Holy War was about to begin. They caste lots for the gun. None had enough faith to trust God's power alone to make Reveered miss.

The odd boy out went coatless to Execution Stand; to the sacred spot where music played. It was cooler tonight and the sharp air stood his skin on edge. Once there, with only three teammates separating him from the Heathens down the hill on the other side of the creek, he pushed the boombox PLAY button and started tonight's Holy War!

The boy looked at the stereo, frowned and reached his hands up. He took hold of the rope that hung from a thick branch jutting out from the old oak and started singing the AGA theme lyrics of Holy War. The boy's voice drifted across the land as he sang along with the song, *Jesus Freak*.

> *Separated, I cut myself clean*
> *From a past that comes back*
> *in the darkest of dreams*
> *Been apprehended by a spiritual force*
> *And the grace that replaced*
> *all the me I've divorced*

Three boys ran down hill.
War was upon them.
"Hey Luke!" one whispered.

Holy Rollers & Highwaymen

"Shhh. Reveered'll get us!" Then the three went stealth and crept toward the creek, holding to soft ground of the lowland to avoid the crispy leaves of the big oaks. Like they would fall for that again. Clinging to shadow as best they could, they moved forward, flanking toward the heathens where the candles burned. And the waiting guns.

Luke held up his fist as if a Seal team captain.

The two following boys took a knee and all was still and calm. They could hear gurgling creek and coyotes howling and yapping to the north.

"You scared or something, Luke?"

"Yea. Reveered wants my soul for shooting Angie last week!" Luke said in a low voice.

"And you'd still rather kill? What card do you have? The same as last week when you shot her?" a boy whispered.

"Hey. God is life! He'd want us all to live!" Luke said, holding up his card and looking at the others as he swung the barrel at them.

They all held out cards.

"Okay! No wild card!" Luke said.

"Let's stop eating American Crap, Luke, and chuck the gun this time! Murder is not in our cards or the Bible."

"Killing in self defense ain't murder. Let's keep it just in case," Luke said.

"Why can't we just love our enemies, like the card says?"

"We can. We'll only waste them in self-defense."

"Reveered's gonna waste us if we don't shut up!" the third said. "He's the Dark Horse of the Apocalypse!"

"Let's wait right here!"

"Yea right! And hang Stand Man with no attempt to rescue? We're all going to be in his spot in minutes. Game or no game! Let's get the shield, man, and get back across the stream. They can't shoot us all!"

As he said this, they all rubbed their arms.
The shooters could indeed shoot them all!
But the boys nodded for bravery and crept forward towards the light.

The melody from the boy behind them, up at Execution Stand drifted across the dark land to where the boys were strategizing.

Kamikaze, my death is gain
I've been marked by my maker
A peculiar display
High and lofty, they see me as weak
Cause I won't live and die
for the power they seek!

Boys looked at each other as the voice of their friend defied and taunted the tolerant by song and creed.

A boy came alongside Luke and whispered. "We gotta get the Bible! It helps me. You know, it helps me when I'm standing to know your risking it all to get your hands on The Shield! I can imagine it a real shield when I'm standing." The boy rubbed his chest where he had gotten pelted last week.

They stopped when they saw the Stone Table through leafless branches. But at fifty yards, they couldn't see the Bible on it, but knew it was there. And they knew it was surrounded by more than just flickering candles.

The song played on.

The Christians had the length of the song to steal the Bible and get it to the Stand Man before the martyr got pulverized in a mock execution to win Holy War. The three variables were wildcards, the Heathen defense and Reveered. Their friend sang out loud and off key. He had more courage than last week. Practice was making him perfect.

People say I'm strange
does that make me a stranger?
That my best friend was born in a manger!

Boys left shadow, creeping towards the Bible.
"They're waiting to draw us in?" Luke said.
Reveered's saw them come up close to him and his smile nearly changed the current.
The boy's paused. "Maybe all the Heathens went to kill the Martyr. Maybe no one is there and we're wasting time?"
"Should have stayed in your catacombs," Reveered whispered, his breath fogging white over cold water. Sheople were in the open, moonlight reflecting off their head gear.
Melody drifted across wasteland as the one awaiting martyrdom worshipped in song. Fear was getting to the singer now. He was going more off tune, anticipating getting shot.

People say I'm strange
does that make me a stranger?
That my best friend was born in a manger!

Reveered lifted his paintball hopper out of the stream, careful not to rattle icy balls and attached it to his weapon. Under water-gurgle cover, he chambered a round and brought the barrel online with Luke's leg. But when Luke scratched his chest with a bare hand, temptation was too great and Reveered squeezed the trigger, aiming for the sensitive nerve endings in the exposed finger tips. His gun jumped.
Some balls thudded the hand in violent impact, but one slipped in under Luke's chin protection and sunk into his neck.
Luke dropped like a beheaded missionary then Reveered

nailed the others, knocking one into the creek with a splash.

"Jeeze! Reveered!" a boy gawked, holding his burning arm and looking down at Luke. "Nice shoot'n!"

"Killing a Christian is nothing to be proud of yet," Reveered said, slipping off Luke's helmet and tapping the boy's cheek. He beamed a flashlight on the injury and wiped paint off Luke's neck. Light showed a dark bruise on the neck the size of a silver coin.

Luke started to cough.

Three Heathens, hearing Reveered's gunfire, then charged Execution Stand. "Shut your fool mouth!" Angie yelled. Others called out too as they took the hill, martyred the defiant singer at Execution Stand and shut down his music.

His pain scream carried a different tune.

"Over here!" a boy yelled. "Holy War's over!"

The girls gathered at the river.

"We gotta fix these helmets," Reveered mumbled as Luke was resurrected. "We're going to have to cancel the rest of tonight until I fix these masks to make sure we really *don't* kill someone. Let's head up to Martyr Hill."

They climbed and set fire to dried branches and leaves in the firepit up near Execution Stand. They sat near the rope that dangled from the thick, outstretched limb of the oak.

"If it ever comes down to being burned at the stake," Reveered looked at the seven as the fire flared up, "Inhale the smoke and pass out. Fire is a tough way to go."

"Aren't all ways hard?" Luke asked with ice on his neck, watching sparks go up into night sky and faces of his friends all aglow in firelight.

"Some more than others. Read *John Foxes Book of Martyrs* if you want to see the imagination of the dark heart of man. Read the thick one, not the thin one." Historian, sociologist and now theologian, Reveered went on to talk about the irreconcilable war between God and Satan, and how battles happen wherever people of conscience offend a culture that has buried its guilt.

Jones Watson's cronies borrowed the car from a Tremble Alzheimer grandma who didn't know she had a garage, and sprang the trap in downtown an hour before midnight. Their plan hinged on a fluffy dead cat, which they bounced off Maybell King's windshield. It thumped off and she stopped, holding true to profile.

A fake bearded boy with gray hair had pulled over too. He kneeled over the dead cat.

Maybell stepped out. "Oh no! Oh no!" She left her car and knelt beside the cat. "Is it okay?"

"Let me check." The thief put an ear to its chest then lifted an eyelid to check pupil dilation.

"Can we take it to the Vietnam Vet?" Maybell King wanted a miracle.

"Its time has come."

"Are you sure?"

"Yes. It's passed away." Since he was the one who had wrung its neck earlier, authority filled his voice. He held the cat near asphalt behind Maybell's seat and listened to Maybell sobbing. He put a hand on her shoulder. His other fingered up the door locks.

Ace observed the robbery as Maybell stroked at the cat. It took 12 seconds to replace the money in her bank bag with replica bank envelopes filled with paper napkins and iron scrap.

A full minute passed before Maybell calmed. Watson was nervous from his perch two blocks away, holding a big cockroach on the lens of Tremble's only roof mounted camera on the 7-11.

"I'll take her home an bury her proper," the California Kid said. Deft fingers placed the cat in his backseat and closed the door. Knowing a crime scene is never a good place for a camp out, Ace climbed behind the wheel, rolled down his window and closed the door on Maybell.

"Are you okay?" she asked walking beside his moving car like a Secret Service agent would a president.

"It's hard. I love cats." Ace said and started to roll faster, making her stop, winded. Ace waved and watched Maybell King stand defeated on Main Street in his rearview mirror. Once around two corners, Ace chucked the cat out the window, returned the car and joined in the counting of loot.

The darkness around the convent was as calm as medieval forest. Deer were grazing nearby when their ears twitched and their bodies tensed.

The scream again.

Deontra's mom held a cool cloth to her daughter's burning forehead. Sisters prayed the Rosary at the victim's request, then sat in silence until the girl drifted into another twitching sleep.

Sunday was a day away. The priest would then meet Deontra.

The Sisters prayed for him to have courage to speak order into *this* kind of chaos.

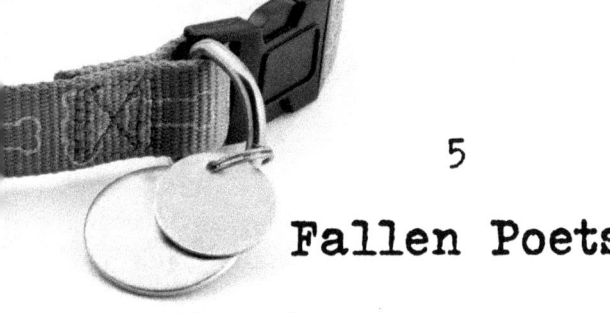

5
Fallen Poets

Riders on the storm
Riders on the storm
Into this house we're born
Into this world we're thrown
Like a dog without a bone
An actor out alone
Riders on the storm
            -Jim Morrison

An ill wind, a fowl-smelling east one, blew across Michigan, prodding Tremble's leaves into the river west of town. Rain was imminent as Nesters scurried up the concrete face and got under their overpass. Nesters loved their perch.

Tremblens endured Nesters and their Bridge Art because it showed the trouble waters of area youth and how subcultural perversion and pain was upon them. Nester Slope was the long cement incline under Hwy 10 Bridge over the river in downtown Tremble. More often than not, it canvassed the nasty.

Passing under on the River Walkway, one saw many crude words and vulgar pictures. Noose ropes hung under the bridge like vampire traps.

Mothers pushing strollers *never* paused there. Tremble City Police posted signs and tried to flush out the artists, but Nesters are truly bird like in resiliency and hadn't given up their territory. They had passion for their turf plateau because they were ambush predators. Briars and barbwire crowded the nest on both sides and they threw sand on the angled concrete, making the slab, the only entrance to their nest, too slippery for an adult.

Nesters loved their perch, the perfect pad of any decent buzzard. Today their talons had snared Suzan Windstop again. She could cut a hole in a farm blanket, stick her head through, shake out thousands of her curly blond hairs and make it fashionable.

Susan could make anything fashionable. And she did. "Spam's down there again," she said and boys like hatchlings peeked over the edge.

Even bad weather didn't change Spam's route on Saturdays. It was the day he visited the gravesites of his parents and brother. And to do so, he had to pass under Nester's Bridge. By doing so, he defied the Nesters. To Spam, receiving Nester abuse was penance. A time for him to remember what he had done to his brother on that fateful Saturday seven years ago.

Spam approached.

Nesters targeted him.

Spam walked closer, keeping his eyes to the river. Circles in the sky were on its surface because rain. A trout took a fly and he saw more ripples spread across the gray-clouded reflection. Atmosphere came in and out of focus as submerged rocks displaced water. Then Spam lifted his eyes to Nester's Perch and pulled at Susan's gaze, as if the two of them were connected by string.

"Hundred bucks if you can get him to talk," a bird said.
"No way. Even Suzan can't!"
"True?"

She nodded, hiding her hypnotic eyes from them as she stared at Spam. "I try every day. I think he's more than most."

Nesters looked at each other as if they had just gotten their wings clipped. Pecking order time! They measured distance and took up ammunition. Heads tilted to gauge velocity.

"Spam'll never learn."

"I'm going to nail him this time!"

"Spamity Spam!" One chirped.

"Bombs away!" another yelled and their missiles took flight. With good trajectories, all projectiles arced along bridge beams before making their descent.

Three splashed in the river, but they chirped at the fourth. It wasn't big or sharp, just an egg-size stone, that thudded off the top of Spam's skull.

Spam fell into mud, but managed to hold eyes with Susan as he wobbled back up like a chipped Weeble.

Nesters squawked and flapped their wing-like hands in conquest.

Another routine Spam bombing complete! Everybody knew Spam couldn't rat. His drunken dad had broken his voice box. Easy pick'ns.

But Suzan was still looking down at Spam as Nesters stretched their wings. She saw tears. "Spam's crying," she said.

A boy waddled back to the edge and opened his beak. "Spam you freak! You gonna talk this week?"

Suzan shuddered.

Spam watched Susan until the Nesters pulled her out of sight. The gash bit hard into frayed nerves and he wondered why he was able to cry. He hadn't wept since before the fire. Blood was warm on his scalp and red on his face as the wound bled out. It used to take effort not to flinch, but that last stone had knocked something lose. It had been a seven years since he had wept. A smile cracked on his face. The muscles around his mouth felt awkward, unexercised. Uncoordinated. Maybe it was happening.

Across town, in an upstairs bedroom of a small white house, Wendell felt warm and good. Inside his head, logic got foamed by what felt like pasty, gray lard. Thoughts went unchecked as his brain's tectonic, sanity plates, rumbled aftershocks.

He saw Deontra come to him with ocean power and sunrise life. "Protect me, Wendell," she whispered to him again.

Then he watched her get clubbed and beaten over again and again as his merciless mind kept replaying the rape until his eyes went windowless. His ears, ripped open by her gasps, seemed to drip blood. Knowing how the hounds had bit into her throat, made *him* gag until acid swirled in his mouth and started rotting his teeth.

The mental storm passed, having ravished most of his Saturday as he stared beyond the wall, inches in front of eyes. The wall then came into focus as he heard the weeds of Rape Field whispering.

He then knew he would kill four rapists.

What he didn't know, and by definition couldn't know, was that he was going insane.

When Carp saw Spam he unloaded a dog from the metal table. It hit the floor in a claw scratching thump, and Carp tapped the warm spot.

Spam stepped up.

"How were the gravesites?"

"I didn't go."

"Because the Nesters?" he scrubbed in.

"No. Not really. I just didn't."

"Interesting!" Doc focused the operating light on blood-matted gash. "Glancing blow. No stone bruise. Get it?" He flipped on the electric razor and doused rotors with a clear liquid, flushing varmint hair into the sink. "This stuff," he sloshed the bottle, "will kill everything this time!" He shaved hair from around Spam's wound and scrubbed dried blood off skin and stitched scalp. He finished by splattering on some home-brew antibiotic goop that was as dark as tar, but dried on contact.

Then they went and sat in their recliners.

"I felt today. I'm starting to feel," Spam said.

"For who?"

"I don't know."

"Nesters?"

"Everyone. I cried."

"No shame in that. Sticks and stones sting."

"Wasn't that."

"Really?"

"The fire. I felt its heat," Spam said.

The man threw a metal spoon at a dog chewing on the magnetic strip of his refrigerator. "Takes a long time."

"Then some."

"Why is that?" Carp asked.

"Look at me. Look what I did."

"Your mom suicided because of you?" Doc tilted his head as if the back of the chair was flypaper.

"Ya. Probably," Spam said.

"That was nice of her. Your drunk Dad?"

"You're right."

"You're darn right I'm right! And now you mourn your brother after these long years?" The vet picked up a cat by the scruff, held its mouth open with the butt of a nearby pencil and inspected the cyst on its tongue. "Do you know what I think?" Carp asked, dropping the cat.

The boy saw his friend. The man's passion for battle was the essence of their friendship.

Off went the cat.

"I think you broke your seven-year silence," Carp said.

Spam blinked. More tears came. He felt them drop off his cheeks and land on his shirt as if they were diamonds.

6
Killdeer Was Here

Gene Thompson hated Tremble's farmers because they mocked his family land. He hated his mother too, because she sold off over 700 acres when he was too cheap to pay her pennies on the dollar for it.

"Why should I pay you?" Gene had said to her when she was near her deathbed. "I'll inherit it soon enough!"

But Ms. Thompson didn't die. Instead, she up sold the land to Dr. Carp, Tremble's Vietnam Veterinarian. "That soldier has old school spunk and I like men with sand, unlike you and my other worthless off-spring!" She had told Gene.

That hurt.

His mother's words cut him deep. So Gene hated the town's basket case, Vietnam baby killing land swindler. That was decades ago. Time passed but the hate didn't. It festered inside Gene's soul.

Gene hated financial mistakes and the one he made with his mom was the big one that still ate at him. He was still a landowner. One of Trembles largest with over 2,000 acres. He paid a dirt farmer, Peter Mongrel, to seed 80 acres to stay qualified for government subsidies and agriculture tax breaks. But Gene had taste for finer things and ranched some tasty heifers. He sold the meat to hide his cash cow.

Gene Thompson's public money came from his teaching job at Tremble High. He taught four classes of Senior Government and one Gifted Government class at Tremble High as well as one lousy sophomore Government class that was pretty much a waste of time. But he was so much more than an instructor; he was a friend to the friendless and an inspiration to the apathetic. And if one had access to the flow of money at his fingertips, one would see an annual cash income just over 1.2 million. That's because Gene was Tremble High's sole drug care provider. Of course he couldn't deal at lunchtime like Elementary Education teachers did Ritalin. Gene wasn't state certified.

Back in '70's, when grass was green around all fences, Gene had found a loyal teenager. That kid soon got eight peer leaders nibbling. After a few lucky months, Gene found himself influencing a lot of student money. His puppet leaders had some problems with cops in 1978. Parties got crashed and High Times were changing, so Gene offered up one of his old barns, so his buyers and sellers could party in peace. It was his dirt farmers idea. Peter Mongrel had some good memories in barns back in the day.

Then the '80,s Drug Tzar powered up. Cops got helicopters to scope out Home Grown, and laws came, making it tough for Gene. But Peter had a second idea. While plowing a hillside, he had discovered a cave, a sort of geological wonder. Overgrown with weeds and scrub, it was volcanic glass. A bit of an anomaly, really, the best Gene could figure was that something big, like that Yellowstone Caldera eons ago, barfed up a chunk of rock and heaved it half way across the continent. The ride hollowed it with holes like Swiss cheese until in splashed into a Great Lake or glacier or whatever else was covering Michigan at the time.

Frankly, Gene didn't care, he was too busy building the areas first hydroponic subterranean. With the right lights and a generator, he started growing Michigan Pure Hybrid Marijuana 24-7. No electric bills. No infrared threat. And no detection from whirly birds. It was like Disney World; he harvested money year around! Only he didn't farm it. His first student leader did.

Peter Mongrel had a bit of a green thumb. And he wasn't into power. He just got paid off with unlimited homegrown pot. So Peter lived life open air dirt farming by day and blue haze, Led Zeppelining pot at night. It was a perfect world. Over the years, he spawned off a couple of kids with some of Tremble's tramps. All in a days work. They had all grown and moved on. Except one. His youngest. He had named him Sid, after an elk hunting guide in Wyoming who helped him take down a six by six, but most everyone now just called his boy, Mutt.

Mutt, like a few other teen leaders had been virtually hand-picked by Gene from birth. They were introduced to him early on by parents, his former clients who still liked the habit. By tradition and honor, leaders came to Gene from their ancestors. But they still had to distinguish themselves in case the apple fell far from the tree, so Gene groomed them in ways that made them grow up quick.

Gene would never grant leadership on blood relation alone. He made them prove merit to build confidence. And re-prove it when he had the urge. Gene was a government teacher, not an equal opportunity liberal.

Through the decades, the sizzling rumor that Gene manipulated was Sacred Keg. The whisper of the perfect party in hallways was so soft that the daily buzz droned it out. And the years when it did rally witch hunts? Mr. Thompson scaled down, posted No Trespassing signs and diverted flow to partners, now parents, former ringleaders.

Gene's whisper kept the ideal of Sacred Keg alive. So elusive was this rumor that co-workers saw it as far-fetched as the Holy Grail. In 30 years, there weren't more than 50 odd souls who could finger Gene Thompson. And now with his 16th generation of Sacred Keg guardians in place, Gene started to relax. Having placed members in City Police,

County Sheriff and City Council. He knew where enforcement was looking before they did.

Yup. Mr. Gene Thompson ran tap on Sacred Keg and helped the party elite surf the endless summer of sex, drugs and rock-n-roll.

But Gene was getting older and more eccentric. His hair was receding and wrinkles getting longer. He was also sponsoring charities and foundations and was toying with endowing The Thompson Memorial Farm Scholarship to insure his role in shaping the 2020 Tremble Vision. Through the Rotary Club, he influenced plans for the new High School. He had just the place picked out. He had the name chosen too. All he had to do was to drive off the squatter.

During the movie, *Kelly's Heroes,* Dr. Carp's scalpel abused animals because he got laughing at the hippie controlling the Sherman Tanks. Doc should have been sued for malpractice a dozen times over. Fortunately for Carp, his clients were poor linguist. On more than one procedure, Spam had killed the TV to protect the innocent and faced Carp's wrath.

So when Spam entered the clinic and saw the film climaxing, he waited out the fire fight because he needed all of Carp's concentration. Patience is vital when one has a Vietnam Veterinarian for a shrink. Spam learned that in his early days of bootcamp, back when adolescent counseling in Tremble meant having a different reading teacher at school. Back when his Dad started drowning himself 12 ounces at a time and his mom drove away to her final happy spot without leaving the garage. In a way, Spam's parents prepared him well for Carp's Combat Therapy. Seriously, who could make him worse?

Now the boy was nervous. His tangled mind was going

under Carp's scalpel again. Spam was going to vent a happening from last summer.

The movie ended. Clint Eastwood divided out the Nazi gold bars and Carp rolled up his sleeves.

Spam then noticed a dog was going to be in his therapy circle. He'd fit right in.

"Spam, I gotta cut the foot off Byle's poodle. Gangrene all over. It's gonna take a while."

"Good. There's something I need to tell you anyways."

"It stinks like war. You don't have to stay."

"You try the maggot thing?"

"Ya, but I still can't get it right. They breached their borders again."

"You gonna drug 'im or do I hold him down?"

"They paid for the gas, but the little guy's weaseled into the goody box and had more than popcorn during the movie. That's him there," Carp pointed. "The one going around in circles."

"Isn't that because the limp?"

The Vet tilted his head, angling his crew cut, flat top hair as if he needed to roll a marble off it. "No. He'd be circling the other way."

Midway into major cutting, Spam started. "You know the counsel camp they sent me to last summer?"

"Ya."

"Well it was stupid. So I skipped out and walked around the city."

"You're learning."

"I went into this one church. The place was packed."

"Maybe you're not."

The dog winced in pain despite its stoned stupor as greenish juice squirted onto Spam's arm.

"Sick."

"You know that was bothering him!" Carp said as he folded back more skin and flicked out a maggot. Making precise cuts through the tissue and ligaments, he motioned for Spam to continue.

"Well, there was this guy on stage getting everybody all excited."

"This a religious thing?" Carp pointed his bloodied scalpel at the boy. "What'd I tell you about those things?"

"Will ya listen?"

"Lead on Oh Spam Eternal!" Doc went back to cutting.

"This guy was looking for prophets."

The surgeon's shoulders slumped. "You know that before you went?"

"No. He just said so about a hundred times. Then he frenzies through the crowd and points at someone, like they were the one he's been looking for since the dawn of time."

Carp clanged a scalpel into the metal tray a little hard and it zinged out onto the floor.

Agent Orange took it up in his mouth and wheeled off.

Carp took some wadding to stop the bleeding. Then he gave Spam the look. "Plug the saw in will you?"

Spam sensed Carp's discomfort.

Sawbones waved the blade for Spam to continue.

"Well, the guy was yelling away, 'God lead! God show me!' Stuff like that. And when his fingers touched someone, the spotlights beamed on the chosen one and that person got ushered up onto the stage."

"Huh?"

"Then the preacher guy came to my area…"

"…Hang on for a minute. I gotta cut this bone and bleed the tourniquet or we'll lose this furball. It's a timing thing." The whirl of saw blade whined and red bone dust filled the air. The Vet nodded to Spam as he put the spinning blade on the tray.

"He was a couple dozen rows away when he looks dead at me."

"You're a prophet?" Carp asked.

"He stops cold, ice cold, and yells, 'I'm blind! God just made me blind!'" Spam and Carp stared at each other. Spam broke off their trance. "He just keeps yelling it, only he wasn't just making noise like before. He was scared. Scared stupid. People knew it. It was awful."

"You don't screw with God," the Vet said as he removed the tourniquet and medicated the blood flow coming from the bone stub. "You don't want to learn that one the hard way. What *happened*?"

Spam scratched his head.

"Spit it out," Carp said.

"Hundreds of people were between us. I whispered and he heard me. His dead eyes saw me and he heard me, Carp."

Dr. Carp picked up the rotten dog leg, dripping putrid liquid, looked to throw it, then slammed it back on the table. "What did you say?"

"Hey, I said I only whispered it."

"What?"

"Claws will cut. Teeth will bust. Spines will crush."

"Why'd you say that?"

"I don't know."

"What happened?"

"He repeated it! He yelled out, 'Claws will cut! Teeth will bust! Spines will crush!' Then he went into convulsions. Puked all over. And a bunch of men came and took him away."

"Then what?"

"Janitors came and mopped up the vomit."

"Not with him, with you?" He picked up the leg again and pointed it at Spam. "What happened with you then?"

"Nothing."

"Nothing?"

"Well nothing really."

"Really?"

"Well, there *was* this little girl and she knew my name."

Doc spiked the leg down on the metal table again. Only this time it splatted off, slapped up against the wall and dropped into a trash can. He wrung his hands on a towel and glanced at the sink, but spoke anyways. "What did she say?"

"She said, 'Preach questions.'"

"You sure?" Carp kept his eyes down when he spoke.

"What's it mean?" Spam asked, but the man's mind was far away and not coming back anytime soon.

Ron's SUV undercarriage rolled football sized rocks as it kept grounding out on the newly carved road and he snuck a nervous glance at Pamela. Beneath interwoven, leafless branches all was dark and his headlamps bounced from bumps, making it hard to focus.

"It'll be all right," Ron said again. "Trust me."

"Where are we?" Pamela leaned towards him, wary of tree limbs that scratched her window as if they wanted to touch her face. They went downhill and fog came and cut vision. They could see just a few yards of road, which now appeared to be only a two track.

"We're at the right place," Ron pointed. "There's tracks in the dirt." Suddenly the road dead-ended into a brush pile and Ron had to stop, he looked to see if he could turn around, but trees sandwiched them in. They looked at each other. The nearest county road was 15 minutes back and Ron knew his girl was scared. Frankly, he was too. Dark tint on his rear window would make backing up embarrassing.

Killdeer Was Here

An open hand slapped the windshield infront of Pamela and something squeaked scratch marks across it leading toward the passenger side door like fingernails on a chalkboard.

They both jumped and Pamela startled a scream as something else came alongside her window.

They were on both sides of the car, but a lone claw twirled downward beyond Pamela for her to lower her window.

"Don't!" Ron whispered.

"It's him!" Pamela tried to be calm and lowered the window.

"Unlock your doors!" the whisper came.

Rod pushed the button.

A creature opened the door behind Pamela and peered inside.

Pamela knew they were just masked people, but Tremble had some pretty creepy people. The door slammed shut. Then *it* came alongside Pamela's open window and extended itself, crossing her threshold. Pamela saw things like sharpened white bones jutting out from each finger like an organic Freddy Kruger.

"What do you want?" Pamela asked. She put her finger on the window button. Being halfway down seemed too low.

The scare mask came closer. It smelled of leather and fur. It wasn't from Halloween USA.

She didn't like it.

"Lower the window all the way down!" It hissed. "All the way down."

She looked at Ron who lifted his shoulders.

He hadn't heard.

Pamela looked and was horrified by the mask. Clumps of brown hair with white and black tips were shedding off the hide. Droopy deer ears were bent wrong.

It came closer. She felt warm breath and saw human eyes inside the slits where the eyes of the animal used to be.

Ron didn't know what to do.

As if it were reptilian, cold claws snaked under Pamela's hair and the grating click of bones along the back of her neck iced her.

Then came the whisper again, for her right ear only. It came out from under a collapsed, black snout of what used to be the nose of a white tail deer. Long whiskers sprung out from the flared nose and poked into Pamela's cheek. The deer eyes were hollowed out and sunken.

"Nice job on Deontra, Pamela! You got Sacred Keg Style!" The voice was but a vapor behind the scare face. Then it was gone. Something lingered that upset her, but she brushed it away with a hidden drive that cleared her mind and blocked away thoughts and smells.

A boy pulled off his mask and stepped out from behind the brush pile by Ron. It was Mutt.

"Welcome to Sacred Keg!" he announced from the dark. Pamela turned to Ron and broke down in frantic smile.

"Is this really real?" she asked.

"Nice mask! Ron called out to Mutt who must have just slipped it off. "What did you say to my girl?"

Mutt was gone and so was the brush pile.

"He just hissed at me!" Pamela smiled a row of very nice teeth. "We did it, Ron. We're at Sacred Keg!"

A quarter mile later they rounded a corner and saw the barn. Bright lights, mounted in forest, spotlighted it. The slide door was cracked open and powerful blue and red lights strobed. They felt party pulse.

Her fingers tapped Ron's skin for strength. After years of rumor, the barn now loomed, enchanted. Marsh fog drifted in from a nearby swamp and air was rich with moisture.

Moss covered trees were knarred and clicking dead branches as the couple walked down the path past a lone stone hearth that seemed to have grown from a flat patch of land. As instructed, Ron placed a $50 in the nest of money in the big, dented old keg and they entered.

Dozens of teens stopped and looked at them, music lowered and others went still. Two barefoot girls stopped dancing on the roof of a stolen police car.

"That's the cop car that The Keg ripped off seven years ago!" Ron whispered to Pamela, not wasting time to flash knowledge.

It had been rumored that there was such a place. A haven of sorts. A land where no division was between peer groups. A place where only the worthy were equal. But one *had* to be invited. Pamela and Ron had now arrived. Big German beer mugs were lifted in salute, music was bumped back up, lights faded down and the mob went back to the party.

As a whole, Sacred Keggers fell into three groups, each making concession to identity for the greater good. Artists, the ones too big for conventional school activities, controlled the music. Pamela was led past their blue light mosh zone and into the crowd that wore school colors. Many had colors from other schools. There she got her bearings and focused on the party itself. But the far end of the barn got her attention. It was beyond the horse drawn wagon that housed Sacred Keg, caked a wooden barrel of ice. Ron came back from the keg, blowing beer froth towards her from his huge mug. It was too good to be true.

"Is that. . . ?" she asked.

"That's Sacred Keg!" Ron said.

"No! Over there beyond it!" she yelled over music and he squinted through smoke and dust that glowed when cop lights flashed.

"Where the red lights are?" he asked.
"Yeah. What is it?"
"The Red Light District?"
"What that?"
"Foreigners. You know the…"
"…I thought that, well, it was… You know, gone."
"We're at the Sacred Keg, Pamela! All's alive and well!" Ron smiled to invite another question.

Pamela declined. She knew the name, Foreigner, had derived from two Amsterdam exchange students obsessed with porn sex.

They left years ago, but it was now obvious the practice didn't go with them.

Pamela blinked through the strobes and saw flesh and blanket tangle. She walked closer and felt the soft eyes of some girls.

Ron did too and he was now looking at one in particular, a blond, named Susan.

Pamela reeled Ron back with a forceful kiss.

Ron responded and Pamela's smile broke it off.

Pamela then lost herself in his chest and felt his strong arms. Knowing he was still looking at the Foreigners, she relaxed in his intoxication and realized she would indeed do anything to keep him.

When she awoke from the slow dance, Pamela saw two thick ropes tied off to a high rafter. Their tails brushed the floor. Against the barn wall, under old, rusted, land-clearing tools, boys with different jerseys from other schools groaned in pain. They seemed to be testing bravery and learning how to cope with hurt. Some sat on a few, 100 lb. bags of old farm fertilizer.

Big Frank looked up at them and smiled. He stood and approached.

Pamela felt floorboards bend under his weight.

Frank was the force on Ron's football team's front line. He struck the quarterback's back and bounced Pamela's head off Ron's chest. "Ron Robertson and Pamela chilling out at Sacred Keg! Let's go, Captain!" Big Frank pointed at the ropes. "Winner screws the pooch!" He smiled at Pamela and opened his eyes wide.

Pamela's arms tightened around Ron's neck and she closed her eyes, not wanting to share. Pamela then looked to opposing ladders going up barn walls. Challengers would haul ropes up to the lofts above and swing to a collision.

"Too complicated," Ron said.

"I've never been beat! Tremble owns The Rafter this year!"

"She could take you one-handed!" Ron looked down into Pamela's eyes. "And then I'd have nobody to block for me."

She looked over at Big Frank.

"Where's your manners, Big Frank?" Pamela reached for his beer. "You didn't offer me your drink?"

Frank gave it to her quickly and left to fetch another.

"You okay?" Ron asked.

"I'm at Sacred Keg with Ron Robertson a mere month after our first kiss! Can it *get* any better?" She looked up into his eyes.

His big hands took her body around her ribcage and lifted her high up so she could be eye level with him, and as her arms went around his neck, she kissed him.

She held him tight and felt him dance her around the floor with her feet swinging high off the ground. She leaned her head onto the top of his shoulder, closed her eyes and tried to force away the foul memory of the stretched and disfigured deer face. But something else came with the smell. Something she couldn't just flush away.

It wasn't Pamela's first time at Sacred Keg.

7
Sunday Stations

Wendell Shyly sat in church with about ninety others, but he was alone as he planned the murders. Peace and quiet of sanctuary helped him see soft spots under the hairy hides of the dogs. Here, their claws and teeth seemed duller, their blood not so resilient.

Shifting, Wendell left his notes and scoped for spies. Seeing only *worshippers*, he relaxed, watched the minister move his lips and then resumed his pre-meditation.

Inspiration came.

Wendell remembered crossing Mutt's pissing territory along a row of lockers and how one of the dogs had snarled at him with a weird, bothered look. It prodded Wendell to keep walking down the school hallway, but it also made him turn and look behind him. When he did, he saw the dog's paw give up on the combination lock, smack the door then push something into the locker vent.

Now Wendell lifted his head to the pastor and smiled.

He almost said, 'Amen', at the providence, but suppressed his enthusiasm. Wendell's church frowned on outburst that brought attention to people.

Just over three blocks away in downtown Tremble, Deontra pulled open a heavy carved door, which groaned on iron hinges, and entered the stillness of her stone church. Her eyes adjusted to colors, prismed in thick air from stained glass windows. Vaulted ceilings made her lift her glance up from the floor. The coolness of stone basin holy water stung her warm forehead as she crossed another threshold.

She saw candles flickering at the front of the small cathedral, splashing light on the bronze Christ held to a cross by nails. She saw his ribs jutting out, his outstretched arms and she saw agony on his face.

He knows how I'm feeling, she thought. Nuns sat in wooden pews. If Deontra had focused she would have seen all seven, but it would have been difficult. They seemed to be a part of the structure of the church, masked like hidden images artist draw into pictures.

In the corner, flame burned from a red candle. To some it was a symbol of the attending Holy Spirit of God, to many its light was his incarnate presence.

Her heels clicking on stone floor was the only sound. The stillness of the House was powerful and Father Albertson came alongside and escorted her to his office to the right of the pulpit. Enroute, Deontra extended her hand and brushed it across one of the nuns who sat near candles, praying.

The girl entered a room lined with thousands of books. A round table with two chairs was in the center of the room and a big clock stood in one corner, facing the door like a soldier. The door stayed open behind her, and Sister Sage, Deontra's most trusted mentor, entered and sat by the clock.

The priest pulled out a chair for Deontra and then walked around the table, sat across from her and let his weight settle.

She looked at his library. "Where did you get all these books?" Deontra asked.

"One of them was given to me."

"Which one?"

"The one that shows us how to heal. If you hear its truth, I will lead you in the Prayer of Absolution to make solid your resolve. To weaken the rage that burns in your heart."

"I don't understand?"

"The truth or the rage?"

Fear turned Deontra pale. "I know well the rage. What truth are you talking about?"

"Forgive the boys who raped you, Deontra. Name by name you forgive them before Jesus Christ. Then you love them and pray for their salvation, so they may celebrate the goodness of God with us. Pray for them so they can worship God with us forever in heaven."

The grandfather clock seemed to stop. Silence crescendo came.

"I don't understand?" Tears filled Deontra's eyes, swelling her pain. Her face flushed a shade darker. "I was attacked!"

"And violation is a horrible, violent pain. But it can end, Deontra. Choose forgiveness and start to end it."

"Or what else?"

"Go bitter. Which over time only tortures and destroys. God gives what we ask for. That can include darkness, but when he grants dark prayers no human can stand the torture, Deontra, so the bitter heart becomes the endless victim, an enemy against God's Kingdom. The cynical heart. The hopeless one."

"I *won't* forgive them." Deontra clenched the arm rails of her chair as if it was going to turn upside-down. But it did no good in protecting her from the priest.

Father Albertson rose with resurrection power. "Then you must leave." He walked to the open door and outstretched a hand to Sister Sage. The nun rose, lifted Deontra and guided her back into church.

On Sundays, Dr. Carp slowed the clinic to a reptiles heart beat in a Canadian winter. Most animals had been shipped home, one way or another, and the remaining patients seemed to welcome the structure and settled down, each finding a place to rest. But when the doorbell rang, Agent Orange activated his bark, which shook the clinic walls and got the weekend guest all riled up.

Carp shuffled to the door with his entourage of yappers and opened it.

It was the fuzz.

"Sorry to bother you, Dr. Carp, I'm Officer Brighton," a City Policeman said.

"You the one they call OOB?" Carp looked beyond the flushed man and saw an old woman down the steps. Carp's hand rubbed his whiskers. "Maybell? Why would he be called Officer Oink Brighton?"

Officer Brighton flushed. His big round head went a shade of red. His short hair and Spock-like ears helped him land the name.

Carp opened his door to them. "Maybell, how's your feline family?" Carp asked before they were introduced.

"One's got a limp," she said.

"Bring it with you?"

"Over my dead body will you ever touch one of my cats!" she said.

Carp smiled. "Why can't the whole world be like Maybell King?"

"We're here on a whim, Doc, but Maybell wants to check out your coolers if it isn't too much bother." The officer said with an edge.

"What for?"

"We're looking for a cat. A dead one," Brighton said.

Carp stood back and waved them inside. Over the decades an unwritten civic duty had come to be in Tremble. If you found a dead-something-or-other around town, you scooped or scraped it up and dropped it off in a freezer in Carp's always-open garage.

The three of them took a shortcut to the roadkill deer freezers.

"Any get beaned around Tremble?" Brighton asked.

"Always. Got a few I think," Carp said. "One's pancaked. You mind me asking what's this is about?"

"It's County Fair season, Doc, and the Carnies came calling on Maybell King. They were a mighty smooth using a cat to help sticky finger the football gate money out from underneath her."

"Used a cat as a Mickey, did they?" Carp asked.

"Where are they?" Maybell's fur was up. "I don't cotton to thieving. Next they'll be saying I'm too old to do my job."

"I'll take care of you when that time comes," Carp said. "I can fit you in on any given Friday night." He lifted the lid where small road kill got dumped. He pulled out two cardboard stiff cats and carried them inside by their tails to his stainless operating table and thumped them down on an opened pizza box with a few left over slices.

"You don't want to see the other one," Carp said.

Maybell came close. "Don't need to," she pointed. "That there's the one."

"You sure?" the officer asked, questioning her ability to identify the dead.

"Never doubt what Maybell knows about cats," Carp said. "If she says that's the one, it's the one."

"How'd it die?" she asked.

"Broken neck by the looks of it," Carp said, not liking the look in their eyes.

"Doc? I hate to ask you this on a Sunday and all, and were not asking for an autopsy, but. . ."

"I'm not the one who killed it am I?" Maybell asked, then

Sunday Stations

she explained what happened with the car.

Carp went to the cat and turned it over. Ice chips were melting and its fur became matted and wet. He turned on the surgical light and pulled it down.

"It's got a broke neck." He lifted the cat and pointed. "That ain't normal. Getting hoodwinked ain't normal for a cat either, since you're asking."

"Just tell us about the injury. Can it get that by getting ran over?" the cop asked.

"What's going on?" Carp asked.

"That little thief said I hit it with my car, but I'm thinking it was thrown at me just to make me stop," Maybell said.

"This one wasn't ran over. It you want to see a ran over one, we can pull out the pancake," Carp said.

"Can I ask you to hold onto that one for a week or so in case anything comes up? It's our only lead." Officer Brighton asked.

"Sure." Carp saw them to the door.

Maybell looked at the sign and the bowl of cartridges. "That's not funny you know!"

Behind Carp the light went off and the door closed to the garage and he knew Spam was putting the soggy cats back on ice.

The boy had a knack for staying out of sight.

"Can I make a comment?" Carp asked, standing by the open front door.

"If it's about a cat, the Carnie or the money I'll hear it." The City Officer said.

"I don't know too many little carnies," Carp said. "Aren't they kind of fat from a diet of Elephant Ears?"

"This one wasn't. He was dressed up and all." Brighton said and put his hand on Maybell's back as if to protect her from Carp's insight.

"Stop!" Carp said. "No need to get snippy just cause I called you 'OOB'."

"I beg you pardon?" Brighton asked, "What's your point?"

"Hey, if you police want to think Carnies took the football money that's fine with me. I get paid either way and so do you. But can you explain how a Carnie would know Maybell's obsessed with cats? Think it through, Officer. Your thief is home grown."

"You trying to be a cop?" Brighton asked.

"No. But if you keep acting so stupid, it might encourage me to become a thief!"

Wendell took a Sunday afternoon stroll in the woods and picked poison ivy. Leaves and twigs cracked under foot, branches clicked from wind and he snapped on latex gloves. He pulled out the ivy, root and all, stems and leaves intact. *It's the juice that's the nasty stuff.* His uncle, back on the farm in Pennsylvania had said once. He had once inhaled poison oak smoke when he cleared a fence line.

"That crap got into my lungs from a hundred yards out! And you don't ever want to know what happened!" he had said during a holiday visit a long time ago.

Wendell kept harvesting, and tried to imagine the harm.

He executed the felony Monday morning despite the fact that a dozen cops were around, stinking up the school.

8
Pig Eyes & Curly Fries

Officer Oink Brighten chewed on Carp's advice and come Monday morning, he posted Maybell King front and center at the main entrance of Tremble High School near his Command Trough. He put on his tough-cop face, which seemed to genetically modify his eyes up into his forehead area. His nose and eyes bunched together up there while bacon flab bulged out from under his Kevlar vest. He lowered his chin, used his stare to rattle culprits, and his nose to sniff out the guilty like mushrooms in mud.

"I'll knock each one around with Cop Eyes," he brashed to Maybell, "and you look for guilt. It's a long shot cause we got us some poker players around here."

"Ain't no long shot. If Carp says they're here, they're here. He knows more about sin than any ten men!"

Most students hated Officer Brighton and called him Officer Oink, then they shorted the name to OOB or Double-OB, which stood for Officer Oink Brighton. Thank heaven he didn't have a license to kill. A close look at most of the furniture or walls where Brighton walked would uncover dozens of OOB tags. Students marked his beat to make sure he didn't get lost.

But everybody knew the truth about OOB. When he had goods on a criminal, he flexed fat and paraded the arrested. Him being at Command Trough just meant crime happened over the weekend and he didn't know if he should chew fat or slurp gravy.

The collective body of students went on a mutual quest for information. Most thought nothing of the old lady with OOB.

Maybe it was Take Your Mom to Work Day.

Being too small for a keeper culprit, OOB just growled at wimpy Wendell and let him pass under his interrogation hooves.

Maybell didn't give Wendell a second glance either. She knew he didn't have it in him, despite breaking stride at seeing the cop. Her thief would never miss a beat. Her thief was one heartless son-of-a-female dog, killing a cat the way he did. But she knew Wendell from church and called out. "Wendell! Come forth!"

The boy's heart sank. "Yes'm." He kept his back to the door, dreading proximity to OOB. His heart surged and knees nearly buckled as he got oinked with another glance. He forced his eyes to the floor, but kept standing straight and balanced for Maybell.

"Move over boy! You're in my sight line," Maybell said.

Wendell obeyed.

"So, how's it going for you here? Are you trying to saintinize the heathen?"

"Try'n, ma'am." Wendell said.

"Well that's all the Man Upstairs wants from any of us, I suppose."

"Why are you here, Ms. King? If you don't mind me asking?" Wendell turned to some students but the way they looked at him made swing back and face the woman and OOB.

"Some slippery thieving varmints swiped the Football Money right out from under my sniffer after Friday's game. You know who?"

"No'm." Wendell said.

"Anyone around here drive fancy cars? Wear fancy clothes? Flash a lot of cash?"

"No'm."

"Well then you best scoot on your way. Keep a sharp ear for me. They're cat killers!"

"Yes'm." Wendell complied and left.

"He's a good boy. You needn't worry about him," Maybell said to OOB.

"I never worry about those kind," OOB said. "No need to. It's the ones that never been spanked that waste all my time!"

Deep into hallway traffic, Wendell found himself relaxing and feeling stronger. He felt the hand of God had guided him past OOB. Wendell had gotten his marijuana joint at Outdoor Church Camp last summer, but had been too afraid to smoke it. With surgeon gloved hands he had dissected meat from paper last night, squished out poison moisture from the ivy and soaked it up with hemp. For a while it was sticky, then it dried and he did it again. Every move was planned. If he broke out the same time the pound scum were exposed, it would weaken his chances to kill all four. The itching was horrible too. He had re-rolled the drug. A micro-dab of Super Glue fastened the wrap. Then his gloves came off and he lathered his hands and arms in soap as instructed by *The Family Health Book on Botany*.

Near the middle of hour one, Wendell took a bathroom pass and browsed the dog pit lockers. Then between classes, he confirmed the locker number, coming close enough to a rapist to get growled away. In third hour he contemplated and made his attack during the stillness of fourth period. Using the bathroom excuse again, Wendell left class and slid the laced joint into the locker vent. It tumbled into darkness and rested on a dusty math book. Wendell had to fight to slow himself as he walked back to class.

Everyone ignored him.

By lunchtime the football heist was an attack on Tremble High.

Day of the Dog

Carnies were the enemy of the day.

Cheerleaders mobilized and had already gone class to class, flirting up a fair chunk of change and small bills in five gallon drinking jugs. The big bottles were now too heavy to carry and were being wheeled about on red wagons that had been donated by Tremble Hardware two hours ago. It would take more the carnies to knock over Tremble Pride.

Jones Watson and his criminals eyed those jugs. "A half jug is five hundred," one said.

Watson smiled. "We better pass," he laughed and they fixed PB&J sandwiches. Their loaf of bread was soon gone and home-brought jams were being slid around as they did the makings. They worked the image that showed they were hard-up. They made themselves sandwiches everyday. They wanted to be invisible. Their heist had a few thousand more than they expected and had nearly involved the FBI, but the Concession Stand wasn't FDIC insured.

Watson and his mates looked out the windows, beyond the Michigan overcast, and saw golden sands and aqua seas. Allen Scott and Ryan Knack were of old Tremble families. But it took Watson to get them nibbling on what money could buy. Watson, with Ace Dingle's help, had prepared the trip. The one-way migration of a lifetime.

The breakers off Australia were calling.

Soon the only thing to worry about was protecting their PB&J from dingos when camping in the outback during the season of the box jellyfish.

Across the cafeteria, the Dog Pound woofed down lunch and sniffed around for food to steal. Two of them, named Socks and Shoes, were itching to tuck tail. One called Fran stared at the Catholic Cake. But Mutt put him to rest.

"OOB's playing cat-catcher today," Mutt said. They howled because their secret was still safe. They lifted their tails to OOB, goading the little piggy bank who lost his pennies.

Susan Windstop breezed around Mutt and his table, leaving them sniffing her perfume. She looked over at the boy called Spam, sitting alone a few tables away. "You like that corner don't you, Spam?" She asked and graced by.

Football players opened their huddle to her. She was seated and receiving her first round of compliments from the jocks when it occurred to her that Spam had said, 'Yes'.

Four tables away, Wendell sat near the church sheople. He bowed his head before lunch, and prayed that a dog would dig up the poison-dipped bone. Wendell opened his eyes and started eating his burrito, unawares that a puppy called Shoes had found the joint or that it had helped the dog have its day.

Shoes soon trotted into the parking lot, hopped into Sock's car, slouched below the dash and pawed the cigarette lighter. One of the very quiet secrets about being around Mutt was the constant flow of weed.

"Get this," Socks said. "Someone racked the cash from Friday's game. You know what I'm say'n?" he bobbed his head. "Thirteen thousand dollars!"

Shoes flared his nostrils, putting red coil to white paper. "OOB couldn't find his tail in a box of curly fries," Shoes said.

"It's what I'm saying."

"Mutt thought that tasty biscuit ratted us out!" Shoes inhaled and passed the joint.

"She sure was a tasty treat! I can gnaw on her rawhide for a week!" Socks said, inhaling deep and holding smoke in his lungs.

Shoes and Socks should have known the difference between good grass and bad. But they didn't care.

The poison ivy they inhaled into their lungs and blood stream didn't care either.

From below the dash they peeked at the priest who had just parked in the visitor spot.

The man of cloth stepped out, looked around, then entered school.

The two boys looked at each other, the car floor, then dragged the drug until it was done.

Deontra, alone in the crowded cafeteria, faked a smile as her priest came and sat.

"Thank you for calling me, Deontra," the priest said. He had a kind face and a gentle spirit. But the way he had just cleared out students around him made him feel like Jesus whipping thieves from the Temple.

But Wendell wasn't afraid of no priest. He knew he was one too. He could go directly to the Throne Room of God because The Veil was ripped asunder 2,000 years ago when Jesus died on the cross for the sins of the world! Wendell slid a few stools closer so he could hear better. He backed himself up to them.

"Take me home, Father?" Deontra asked.

"Where do we sign out?"

"Let's go now! I'm so scared! What should I do?"

"Did you involve these police?" he asked, frowning at one of the officers in the lunchroom walking his way.

"Could they help?"

"They can't remove the fear that has dethroned God and wants to own your heart."

"Police can't help me?"

"Social justice can't heal spiritual injustice."

"I thought that was just a Sunday thing?"

"Yesterday, today and tomorrow are the same until enemies are forgiven."

Wendell got up and walked away, assured more than ever that no one could help Deontra except him.

OOB wallowed around the lunchroom still on task, only glaring at the students not looking at him. He didn't have a category for a professional thief. Officer Brighton then came up to the priest. "Anybody confess to stealing a bunch of money, Father?" he asked.

9
Plop, Doc & Cop

In his last hour of Tuesday school, Shoes pawed at his ear and heard a dull *plop* as some sinus pressure broke loose. Feeling better, he flexed his jaw and turned his head only to realize a warm watery fluid was seeping out of his ear. Gook ran down the side of his face. It was in his porn beard, oozing downward like warm, marching ants. It dangled off his chin and dripped on the desk.

Pressure came back. His right hand cupped over his ear again and he flexed his jaw, filling his fingers with more fluid. He went to the bathroom.

The mirror wasn't nice to Shoes. There was no pain or discomfort, but the amount of yellow liquid made him nervous. Back in class with a tissue wadded to his ear, he watched the clock, knowing things always got better when school was out.

This law of absolutes wasn't nice to him either.

Fran coasted his Harley Davidson Sportster to a stop and he and Mutt stepped off and they entered Fran's house on a street where all the homes looked pretty much the same.

Wendell watched from someone's makeshift school bus shelter and decided that he would sink an arrow into Fran tomorrow night.

Doctor Remp's office stood two buildings south of City Hall in downtown Tremble. Huge trees shaded thick grass and big rocks lined both pathways leading to separate entrances. One went to the Well Room for kid's needing things like shots and stitches. It was a non-infection room with non-infected books and magazines. The other door opened to the sick room nicknamed, GCS or Germ Central Station. Dr. Remp was very strict about separating the healthy from the contagious. His Sick Room now held a teenager and a pacing mother.

Dr. Remp knew what ailed most Tremblen kids, but after one look at the lad, he knew a cure wasn't coming soon. He suspected the boy's body was trying to flush something nasty, maybe even a food poison or a stubborn virus, but the boy wouldn't answer any questions so Dr. Remp crossed his legs and watched the kid's ears leak. "It's probably a virus," he said. "And it's attacking your ears because there might have been an infection there for some time. Ear infections are hard to detect."

Then right before him, the boy's fever climbed to 103° and the kid's eyes swelled to little volcano tops.

That was a first.

"You're reacting to something, son."

"No I ain't!" Shoes repeated, and despite his mother's smack, he sat quiet.

The next dozen questions came back the same. But Dr. Remp had a hunch and a bad feeling. He made a rare exception and arranged to visit the boy at home in three hours. He didn't want that kid back in his office.

Shoes was sent home and Dr. Remp washed his hands and arms viciously. He closed down GCS until it could be sterilized.

But when a second mother called Dr. Remp about her kid with identical symptoms, the M.D. ambulanced both boys to the big hospital down in Grand Rapids and was waiting for them when they arrived.

Enroute, he had contacted Atlanta's Center for Disease Control, or the CDC, on his cell phone and they faxed their Infectious Disease Cross-Reference Questionnaire to the hospital as well as some procedural protocols for the Emergency Team to comply with.

The boys and their doctor were ushered into a musty hospital entrance far from the crowded Emergency Room. By then their eyes were oozing both clear and yellow liquids and sores were visible in their nostrils. Pain-stretched tongues were licking goop from under noses. Snot sprayed on each exhale.

Dr. Remp now wore a clear plastic head shield over an industrial face mask. His questions were muffled as other masked persons secured quarantine. They had to move quick. An hour later, Doc read question 172.

By then the boys were in beds, boxed in large, bio-hazard, clear plastic coverings. They both stirred upon hearing 172 and one sat up despite their tangle of wires and IV's. The question made them turn toward each other. Since they could see and heard only in waves, they weren't inclined to lie anymore. Socks and Shoes eyes bulged because mucus was trying to weld them shut. Under quarantine coverings, pressure oozed puss from pinholes in crusted, caked eyes, ears and noses.

Falsehoods were now beneath Socks and Shoes.

Dr. Remp tapped the plastic to keep them focused. "So you *have* smoked cigarette from an unsealed pack?" he repeated.

Shoes and Socks were thinking mighty clear about the joint they burned when they saw the priest. It suddenly seemed to taste different from the others that Mutt handed out. But they had trouble telling the medical team because of esophagus blistering. They did their best to communicate. They scratched at the plastic, gestured and bounced on their beds.

Dr. Remp circled question 172 and finished the rest of the Q&A without any other outburst responses. He concluded that the boys were having an acute reaction to whatever had infiltrated itself directly into their bloodstreams through smoke inhalation. That made sense with the totality of devastation and fit the timeline. He was overwhelmed too, because there were a lot of weird poisons that could be fused into a home rolled smoke.

The boys then destabilized and were given more fluids intravenously as well as more Cortisone™ meds to slow their heart rates.

Dr. Remp called his wife. "I'll be home really late."

"What is it?"

"Some sick boys."

"What's wrong with them?"

"You don't want to know. You really don't." His tone stopped further questions. He ended the call and pulled a chair between the beds and stared at charts. He focused on the laced *marijuana* joint. Sickness could be just starting. He phoned his friend, Police Chief Zimmer.

Officer Brighton, who worked the school beat, had his evening off cut short by the Chief. He was the most overworked on the force because high school shenanigans could keep Tremble's entire police force employed. He used flashers and siren to shoe cars away. Flashers were cool. It was after midnight before Officer Brighton made it to the hospital, but it took only a few minutes for him to contact Chief.

"They ain't doing so good, Chief. One nurse said they might not *make* it," Brighton repeated.

"What's Dr. Remp say?"

Brighton cursed. "None of them here have ever seen the like. It's a poison he thinks."

"Of course it's poison." Chief didn't like vagueness. "What's gonna happen to them?"

"It's hard to say."

"Why?"

"Doc says they gotta sleep."

"Let me get this straight. Two of our teenagers reefed a laced joint and now they're so sick that they can't be disturbed? Since when? You go and disturb them and find out what's what. Since when do you listen to some nurse on a police matter?"

After failing to get any new answers from the doctor, Officer Brighton didn't know what to do. The boys were thrashing plenty and he really didn't want to be next to them in case the plastic gave way and contaiged him.

Alarms dinged and nurses wheeled the boys down the hall toward the expensive machines.

Dr. Remp conceded the If. "*If* they don't react soon," Doc muttered to Brighton, "it ain't gonna be good." A couple of parents were around so they kept their voices low.

"Give me something I can use! Could these dogs die?"

"Who?"

"The dogs. These two are part of Mutt's Dog Pound," Brighton said. "You would know if you were a Vet!"

"Well I don't know! Don't even know what to treat them for! We first thought it was stinger sacks on bees but it's not. We now ruled out acids because their pH is only a little off wack. We just ruled out D-Con and some other stuff because their livers are still functioning. Never seen the like! It could finish them. But don't quote me!"

"Well," Brighton swore, "I got to quote someone to the Chief! If they die we got us a murder. If both die it's a double homicide. It'll make the news! Now, I gotta know!"

Dr. Remp gave him his best prognosis and finished by saying, "I told the parents to stay the night."

Brighton picked up his phone. Those kids were gonna die. "Chief, um, I think they're gonna die."

"Those brats got me outta bed twice in the middle of the night! They better be dead by the time I get there!" Chief Zimmer arrived in 25 minutes. He used the flashers too.

The boys weren't dead, but they seemed to be swirling toward that toilet in the sky.

Chief scratched growth shadow on his chin. Now he squeezed the doctor. "If I call the Sheriff into this it gets complicated. So I must know!"

"Don't do that!" Brighton said.

The doctor didn't have to defend things too much. The boys were crashed on hospital beds covered with biohazard plastic and looked fresh out of an Asian Bird Flu Hot Zone. If they had Class Nine Ebola the treatment wouldn't be any different.

"Whatever's going to happen, is going to happen in the next 24 hours," Dr. Remp added.

"What do we got on paper?"

"Most lab test, toxicology and all the other stuff should be in tomorrow sometime." With boys fighting to breathe though tubes in front of him, Chief started flipping pages on the report.

"You got this out of them?"

"Uh, huh," Brighton muttered.

"Good job, considering how they look," he said. "They're friends with Sid Mongrel? That Peter's kid again?"

"He's scum," Brighton said. "Scum of the earth."

"Where's he at?"

"Dunno."

"Why? They're his friends!"

"I'll make some calls."

"Wait," Chief said. "There's been a warrant out on Peter Mongrel for years. If his kid's in the mix, maybe it will bring him back on the grid. Who's Fran?"

"Their other friend." Brighton shrugged. "They're four. They share the same brain. These two globs pull 80% of the smarts. Fran takes a 19% chunk. Mutt gets the leftovers which is scary because he's the leader."

"So these two belong to a group of four?" Chief clarified, "and Shoes finds a dubbie in his locker and reefs it with Socks. Or the other way around. What kind of names are these? How'd you get this info?"

"That's just the way it is," Brighton yawned. "I can get their real names in the morning if you want. I haven't been able to rap them yet."

A poisoned boy coughed vile, yellow fluid around hoses going down his throat, and it oozed back in. His eyes and nose were volcanoing.

"All right, they're gonna die. It's in their blood." Chief Zimmer concluded, "I'm calling Harry and handing this whole mess to him. And if he wants total control of the investigation, he can have it! Get their car to impound and have the team search it for drug stubs. It'd be nice if we could find a stem and get it to Tox."

"I should have thought of that," Brighton said.

"That'd be nice too," Zimmer left, pushing the door hard. It stuck open and triggered an alarm.

Nurses rushed to close it.

With Chief gone, the doctor and officer looked at each other then back down at the boys on beds. "What's that mean?" Dr. Remp asked Brighton.

"It means he's going to announce to the whole world that

Tremble Police Department can't solve a murder case! You gotta keep them alive. Or else the Sheriff Deputies will force feed us Humble Pie."

10
The Trashman

Mutt and Fran knew something was up 15 minutes into Wednesday morning. They were yanked from class by two cops. They were the brown haired hogs. Not the Brotherhood of Blue.

The tall one did introductions in the hallway. "I'm Detective Smith," he nodded to the other, "He's Detective Weston."

"Like the gun?" Fran asked.

"Shut up! We've been looking for you two since last night."

"OOB eat too much?" Mutt asked.

"Just keep it up," the other said. They went towards the office.

The dogs lagged.

"Move it!" Detective Weston's tone jolted them like a cattle prod.

Mutt and Fran were separated and questioned.

"Who's your friends?"

"How long have you been that way?"

"Where were you last night?"

"You always go where no one knows?"

"Where's your hidy-hole?

"Where's your Man Cave?"

"Where do you get your drugs?"

"How much do you smoke?"

"How much do you buy at a time?"

"Who are your enemies?"

"Who would want you dead?"

"The old man back in town?"

"Ever work with poisons?"

"How much do drugs cost?"

After 45 minutes of pepper, cops brought them to their boss.

"Sit down." Captain spoke, paced and read notes to himself. "Since no one seems to have told you much, I'm here to tell you Socks and Shoes are dying. My name's Captain Campbell. I'm sorry for your loss. I understand they were your friends." He had a stack of medical papers and faxes and was still reading.

Imaginations festered.

Then he dropped a typed written document onto the table, pulled a chair and sat.

"I'm going to translate a lot of this medical material to make sure you understand." The Captain yawned. "I was up all night at the hospital. Any time you want to interrupt, just do so. Not that it'll do much good. This here's just one big stack of bad news."

"Do we need a lawyer?" Mutt asked.

"John Grisham fan, huh?"

"No. We go to Tremble," Fran said.

"We're just here to protect you. Someone seems bent on trying to kill your friends. Who knows? Maybe you're next!" He shuffled papers. "Bleeding infection from all orifices," he dropped the paper after scanning downward. "They're in a bad way! You two seem fine. Anyone try to kill you two? How come you two aren't dead and your friends are. Or nearly so. Maybe they'll pull out and only get busted for possession."

"What's an orifice?" Mutt asked, confused but interested.

"You take Biology?"

"We don't have that here."

"It's a *science* class."

"I think we have *that* one," Fran said.

"Orifices are eyes. Ears. Mouth and nose. The butthole or

rectum. The tip on the wing-dinger. Shoes and Socks are having those areas attacked." He tapped the table with his knuckles. "You need to ask yourselves, *Who would want to kill them? Who'd wanna kill you?* They've been poisoned. The poison is coming out any way it can. And when it comes in contact with air it kind of crystallizes or hardens." He put a cigarette in his lips then remembered he was at school. He let them stare at it.

"A team of doctors and nurses are keeping them alive by slicing off the dried puss with scalpels to keep liquids from sealing and imploding their eyeballs into their brains and killing them."

"They've been poisoned? How?" Mutt asked. He was waking up.

"You're asking us?" Captain smiled, "And we're asking you!" He tapped papers. "They smoked a laced marijuana joint. Now they're in a fight for their lives down at the hospital. Both have air tubes going directly into their lungs because their esophagi are constricting from infected blisters. This is keeping them from drowning in mucus. But if the poison finds an organ it will kill them. Then we have a double homicide on our hands. Then you two will live in our world. A world of trouble."

Mutt and Fran stole glances at each other. "We didn't do anything," Mutt said.

"Since when does that stop us? We're getting ready to nail you two. Go line up some lawyers and tell your parents you are the primary suspects once Socks and Shoes die. Upon their deaths you will become property of the State of Michigan. We know you four howl at the same moon and eat from the same dog dish. Drink from the same mud puddle. We'll whistle for you then. We will call you out until you give us what we want!"

Mutt and Fran looked at each other again.

"We're sharing information. Your turn. What do you have for us?" Captain asked.

"Nothing." Mutt spoke.

"You're Peter Mongrel's kid, right?"

Mutt nodded.

"I hear he's bunking on this side of the state again. We got some questions for him too. You seen your old man?"

Mutt shook his head.

"Well, if you two want to see your friends alive," Captain looked at his watch. "I'd skip outta here and do your visitation. They'll probably die any hour."

Wendell looked at a grammar poster explaining active and passive verbs and saw hope. *It might have happened! They deserve it so bad!* Two puppies didn't come back from the kennel and the pigskins had yanked Mutt and Fran from school! *The Dog Catcher in the sky had finely punched the clock!* Wendell focused his eyes on Deontra and her long black hair. His confidence was coming back.

Do you know that two of your assaulters are now suffering? Do you even know the faces of the evil ones? I know! I gave them an ambulance ride just for you! And after tonight, Deontra, you will know even more!

Twenty-three family members of Sock and Shoes listened to head phones, gamed their cells, read magazines, asked questions and tried to relax. Some even dozed in the hospital Waiting Room. Once they had realized the knots that Shoes and Socks had strung themselves into were very complicated, they began to pace and stare. There were no windows so they just started staring at Mutt and Fran.

All medical staff were quiet about the prognosis. Even Dr. Remp. They all knew the kids were in a puddle so deep that only the head cheese could pass the gas. Knowing this, the nurses were thankful that they were just punky people, only qualified to report good news. Support personnel scurried by, noses to the floor.

So parents, stepparents and grandparents all glared at Mutt and Fran and got those two squirming.

"You're bad friends! You two did this!" a very old woman said from across the room.

"Oh shut up, Granny!" a middle aged woman said, who was likely her daughter.

More cops had just left.

The air thickened with the stink of foul play.

Sadness, shock and disbelief were sucked up the air vents. A slow rage festered in family members. Glares towards the two boys *were* lengthening. The consensus now seemed to be shifting in favor of Granny.

Mutt and Fran squirmed.

Nurses had stopped parading family members by the encased boys because condensation was now dripping down the insides of the plastic. Perhaps it was for the better. Last memories are hard to forget.

The ill boys didn't know they had visitors. They were far away, nose to the ground, following the sweet scent of piss toward the Daisy Hill Puppy Farm.

Upon returning to the Waiting Room, the last group of upset kinfolk looked for enemies to shift blame and displace aggression. As a whole, they chose Fran and Mutt.

Then Mutt and Fran were rescued from the lynchers by a nurse who led *them* to Socks and Shoes.

It was OOB's idea.

They were lead into a room that smelled like an egg-farting, leper colony hiding in a sulfur cave.

Tubes extended from mouths of Shoes and Socks as if each had half swallowed an octopus. Other hoses drained their stomachs. They were blinded by a thick line of yellow crystallized puss that looked like a hard frost had settled where their eyelids should have been. Their hearing came after pressure blew out from ears canals. Out-take air vents removed stale air as fresh stuff was pumped in, but it couldn't stay ahead of the moisture excreted from their bodies. Each sick boy had two masked nurses in full-body hazard suits. A person was there punching information into a small laptop that said CDC in big red letters.

An RN checked the masks of Fran and Mutt. "Go up to that plastic and speak loud. They may still be able to hear you."

When Mutt and Fran skirted the area as if it was a cliff, the nursed nudged them to the edge of the beds.

"Boys!" Her tone boomed like a American trying to make a deaf Frenchmen understand English. She tapped plastic to either improve visibility or wake up the poisoned. "Your two *friends* are here!"

The hand of Shoes lifted and touched the plastic, smudging condensation and Mutt pressed his hand to it. The tortured boy clamped his fingers onto Mutt's hand, stretching plastic and increasing pressure. Behind Mutt, a machine beeping out heart rate on an electronic graph, started blipping faster. Then it slowed to a beat every few seconds as the sick boy's heart weakened, then it flat-lined and a sharp, shrill alarm whistled out.

Shoes died sensing Mutt was near.

Mutt and Fran were shoved into the hallway so hard by the nurses that the carcass of Shoes and his plastic box was dragged half off the bed before Mutt broke off the death grip.

Medical teams scrambled.

Family and friends poured into the hallway from across the corridor. They glared at Mutt and Fran. A different grandmother pointed a zombie-like, withered finger. "Go on outta here! Go on outta here afore we geet you! Ya keeled my ganson ya…!" She melted some paint from walls with her curses.

Fran didn't want to be there. Michigan families were just behind West Virginia and Tennessee when it came to feuding. Blood lust was in their eyes.

When Fran turned to get away, he had to hurry to catch up with Mutt. They jumped on the motorcycle.

Fran hard throttled his Harley against the wind. It swirled him as if a twister was near. Death had chased away sunlight and darkness had come quick. Wind pulled at their bodies and cold night air stung their faces and found ways to get under their leather coats as they fled the city. Car lights blurred by, hurting their eyes. Fran doubted Mutt more with every bump in the highway. *It wasn't right what we did to that girl. You don't touch a good Catholic girl. We shouldn't've messed with Deontra.*

As soon as the bike rolled to a stop at the house of Mutt's mom, Fran killed the engine. "What are we gonna do?" he blurted out from under his beanie size, black helmet.

"Nothing. Not a… We do nothing!" Mutt barked and pulled off his helmet.

"But this is because of what we did to her on…"

"You shut up! Right now! Since when do we talk here?"

"But we gotta do something! Someone…"

"You don't know that! We don't know nothing! Come inside. We'll figure it out then."

Fran didn't like it. He started to take his helmet off but changed his mind. He didn't want to be with Mutt. "What are you gonna do?"

"You'll see. Tomorrow then?"

Fran nodded but didn't believe. He fired the bike engine. "Tomorrow then!" he said and drove away from Mutt's house.

Fran was in sight of home when the arrow struck him above the rib cage under his right shoulder. He was gearing down his bike, so not to slide on some gravel at the end of his driveway when he realized a person was standing in shadow by the trashcan. A bow and arrow was trained on him!

Three of four broad head razors of the hunting tip minced up Fran's meat something fierce. The arrow shattered his shoulder blade and knocked him clean off the back of the bike, which zigzagged for thirty yards until it tipped over by a mailbox and stalled.

But the fourth razor diced an artery and Shyly saw the blood squirt outward, spraying through the slit in the coat and paralleling the arrow before arching downward with rhythms of the fading heartbeat.

Fran's good arm thrashed and the body withered around as if on fire. No sound came because bloodletting went fast, but death circled the dying, enjoying ecstasy torture.

The shooter had to turn away. Time passed.

Wendell had watched the biker come toward him, and had stepped nearly in front of him before releasing the arrow. He didn't prepare himself for the dance of death.

TV and movies seemed to blur over those few minutes. Air was thick with the smell of fresh blood as if it had been vaporized. The blood wasn't dark or thick despite the night. It was more like neon red. It glowed. It trapped all light. It was almost as if it wasn't supposed to be seen by human eyes.

Wendell furled his lip, chilled his eyes and turned back to face the dying rapist.

Whimpering and gushing, Fran the dog was no longer a foreboding, intimidator and beater of girls. The arrow sticking through his shoulder seemed to have changed him.

Wendell notched another because, deep down, he expected to see Fran rise and stumble around a little, maybe try to walk up his driveway or use his phone. Or even pull out the arrow and charge him. After all, it was only an arrow. Wendell had read how arrows were weapons of choice for thousands of years. But that was book knowledge. He never knew it until he saw the velocity punch the rabid dog clean off the motorcycle. Now he forced himself to watch the dog bleed to death.

Blood pooled along Fran's entire body and then oozed down the slant of roadway toward the gutter.

Wendell told himself that he didn't kill a person. Just a rodent that couldn't control his perverted gnaw.

Alone on the empty street, with the front wheel of the upturned motorcycle spinning, Wendell was supposed to ask Fran, 'Who's Bam Bam?' That was the plan, but now he couldn't say a word, let alone approach the carcass. He couldn't tell if it was really dead. All was still except the ticking tire.

Oh well.

Wendell took apart his bow, which broke down into three units and stuffed them into his book bag. He went to his bicycle and laid the extra arrows across handlebars. His right hand covered feathers and broad heads stuck out beyond the left brake. He peddled home indirectly, keeping to pavement.

Fran died on asphalt in front of his house about an hour after Shoes and three hours before Socks or Tommy Smith. Fran died alone.

Wendell had split, knowing a town like Tremble was going to want the killer caught. And he had to kill them all before the job was done. His heart rate was high and came in lurches, but night breeze dried his sweat. He didn't think anyone saw him pass by on dark streets.

Once home, he wished he could take a shower but he didn't want to raise eyebrows. He placed the murder weapon under a loose plank along his bedroom wall. He was prepared to move it later if it started to haunt him. He took a deep breath and slugged his chest a few times. His heart was speeding big time.

Fran's wasn't.

And Wendell wondered if the rapist even had a heartbeat to begin with. He dropped to his bed and stared at the ceiling with his hands behind his head.

He knew he had too much feeling to be a psychopath and too much passion to be a sociopath. He scratched his head and wondered what it would be like to be labeled a *serial assassin?*

11
Dirty Dishes

Spam knew something was weird, because Carp needed help loading deer on a Wednesday. Yes. It *had* been a banner weekend for car-deer crashes and freezers were full. It took a while. And since Carp was deer dumping anyway, he had Spam cage and stack the ragged animals that had been dropped off for disposal.

"You're not hearing me." Carp said to Spam, changing his argument. "I'm not saying *you* need to come. I'm saying, *I need* you to come." So after some convincing, Spam got into Dr. Carp's venison laden truck and was instantly saddened by all the yappers who seemed to be pleading for Carp to cancel their meeting with the Pet Maker.

"Where we going?" Spam asked.

"Widow Thompson Land," Carp said.

"Your land?"

"Yeah." It had only been three decades.

Headlights ate up brown gravel, brown grass and rows of brown corn. They passed under black tree limbs. Seeing a squished opossum, Carp braked, stopped, got out and chucked the carcass into the truck bed.

"No use letting it go to waste," he said.

Spam looked at him but didn't ask his question. They drove on in silence. Then Carp turned onto a two-track. After a few minutes Spam noticed they were driving along a wall, piled high with uprooted trees and stumps. Then it opened to a gate.

Carp stopped the truck, pulled out his .45, chambered a heavy slug and put it back in his holster. "We can't be too careful from now on," he said and nodded forward. "Go open the gate."

Spam stepped out into the night and faced the gate. To his left and right, the fence disappeared into the darkness and he noticed it was well hidden by the wall of stumps that also seemed to go on forever. It was a border far from a road.

Behind him, the truck was only filled with the frozen and dying. Spam didn't get it. He put his hand on the gate and noticed it was more like a re-enforced, chain link, prison sally port with razor wire strung across. Then he heard dozens of animals flee the area, tearing across dried leaves in the darkness. He jumped back.

"Hurry up, Spammit!" Carp yelled.

Spam turned to Carp. Truck lights blinded him momentarily. The boy swung the gate, and blinked off dots, then he saw animal eyes covering the horizon from east to west. He kept blinking. The truck came alongside.

Carp swung the door open. "Close the gate and get in you moron!"

Spam jumped to it and found he couldn't get back in the truck quick enough.

Something was wrong in the air.

Carp smiled, reached under his seat and pulled out another gun and handed it to him. "Happy Birthday!" Carp said.

Spam reached over and took hold of it and looked out the window, shocked by countless sets of eyes that darted away from them. Ahead, on the horizon dozens more beamed like eerie strings of Christmas lights loose in the wind.

Carp locked a round into an identical gun. "These are .22 caliber pellet guns with rifled barrels and really pack a wallop!" Carp said. "But they can't really kill anything as long as we don't get too close."

"What's going on?" Spam asked.

"Trust me! We need to keep 'em fearful of man. It's not safe when they're in big packs like this! I want to hear a yelp every time you shoot! It's for their own good! And for your own good." The windows went down and Carp fired into packs of animals whenever groups of eyes stopped and stared.

So great were the numbers that Spam found himself blazing away. Despite the shooters, animals ventured closer, jumping hard at every rifle pop.

"Why do they keep coming?" Spam yelled, yelping coming from every other shot.

Carp was better. He could get them crying for six or seven seconds. "What's in the back?" Doc asked.

Spam remembered. "You mean they've been eating deer since . . . ?" his voice trailed off.

Carp handed the boy a spotlight. His hand shook as the boy took it. "Go ahead!" the man yelled as they drove on. He was bringing the truck up to speed again on the lane as if he were a stagecoach driver evading a band of robbers.

Spam turned on the light and everywhere it beamed he saw animals. Dogs. Hundreds glowed eyes at him. Too many to count. Spam turned the light off and looked at Carp. "You're a pet hoarder!"

"I don't know what you would call me," Carp said. "But it's getting really wild around here!"

They started shooting again. The bullets and yelping sent the message to stay away from the meat wagon. Then the roving bands of dogs just circled about 200 yards out, keenly keeping out of range as if they had to create a giant whirlpool.

Widow Neddles liked Tremble because it was quiet and

Dirty Dishes

predictable. Even after the loss of her husband, which was something very horrible and frightening, the town itself had helped her heal. There were seasonal festivals and decorations and her friends at the Garden Club had been a big support, rescuing her back from her jilt. Their meeting tonight was especially good. They learned how to prepare bedding around roses to protect them from the hard Michigan frost.

She turned her Buick Skylark onto her street, 9th Street, the one where rows of old maple trees weaved their beautiful branches above the roadway. Then she sighed because she had a sink full of dishes. Well, two glasses and a coffee mug to be exact and she thought about how much she liked her new dish soap dispenser. So when her headlights came upon a body in the road and she realized what it was, she did what anyone her age would do.

Widow Neddles screamed herself stupid.

Not long after her fear of dying was gone, she locked herself in the car and made her first 911 murder phone call and dared again to look at the body. She saw an arrow stuck into torso as plain as a red rose against white fence and she screamed all over again, doing hysterics for the 911 operator.

Officer Brighton was off duty and nearly back from the hospital. Hearing it over the radio, he was the first patrol car on the scene.

"You're detained as a witness," he said, panting.

"Can I go?"

"No."

"I'll testify in court. And you know you can count on me. I'll testify good!" Widow Neddles said.

"He's already dead," Brighton regretted meeting her already.

"But a judge may need to hear it from me!" she said. "I'm silver."

"Get back in your car and stay there! This is a crime scene." He hard stared her toward her car then went to inspect the body. He started cursing. It was one of the dog pound. It was Fran. The boy was as dead as disco. Brighton rolled tape around the area and stepped in his circle.

"Fran! What in the heck did you do?" He walked along the body, trying not to step in too much blood.

Back in the car, the lady was putting her cell phone to good use. Within 20 minutes Widow Neddles circle of friends had dialed theirs and in less than an hour, Tremble knew Widow Neddles had found a murdered boy. And, coincidentally, it made her an honorary expert in homicide and raised her standing as a gardener.

Chief Zimmer zoomed in and saw Brighton inside the tape. He slammed his car door behind him and rushed up. "Get out of the crime scene, officer!" he scolded. "Matter of fact, extended the scene perimeter."

Chief was then the second to question Mrs. Neddles, thanking her for her service to Tremble, then he went to the scene himself.

"Can you believe it?" Brighton giddied as he followed boss inside the tape. "This is Fran! Two on the same day! He's a friend of the mukes at the hospital!"

"How's the live one doing?" Chief yawned.

"Dr. Remp says he won't be topside long."

"I don't believe it!" Chief muttered. "Get Peter Mongrel's kid and quick! We gotta get him safe! Didn't someone just talk to him?"

"County just ran them through the grill at school and then again over at the hospital a few hours ago by the sound of it." Brighton took another yawn and nodded toward Mrs. Needles. "What are we going to do with her?"

"She's a dead-end witness, but we'll let the Sheriff's team

meet her. They'll be here any second."

"Did you have to call them on this one too?"

"Brighton! Don't sound as stupid as your appetite. These are homicides of white teenagers in Smalltownville, America. This isn't a black-on-black driveby over in Flint. People besides Michael Moore are gonna care! And with one of his friends dead of poisoning on the same day?" Zimmer went close to Brighton. "Even if we had the staff, we couldn't handle the pressure. This goes to County Sheriff with pleasure. The media will invade this town like mayflies!"

Citizens became gawkers at the perimeter and Ms. Neddles fielded questions.

Now Tremble's entire Police force of five were standing inside the outer yellow tape and looking very cop-like.

That's when Sheriff Department cruisers screamed around the corner, bouncing more blue and red strobes off trees, front yard mailboxes and houses. The detectives came up.

"Move the tape back 200 feet on all sides and get those people back. Run the tape across the road both north and south of here! No more cars come by, and get those people way back! And you men!" He pointed at Brighton and the others guarding the body. "Get the heck out of our crime scene!"

One deputy recognized the chief. "Chief Zimmer? I'm Deputy Smith," he said and pointed. "He's Weston."

"Yes?"

"We just questioned this boy at the hospital. I knew he was hiding something! Stupid little punk!" The man looked around.

Neighbors were out of houses. Some were looking for Fran's mother. Poor woman. "A parent will be here soon. Set up a human wall. No parent should see their kid like this."

Two more cars, sirens screaming, came into sight and

screeched to a halt. As they cut the noise, more sirens in the distance grew nearer. "Keep your boys out of this area." Deputy Smith said.

"No problem."

"Stick around though, we'll need some help. We'll have to canvas this side of town in the next hour. Who called it in?"

Chief nodded, not used to having orders barked at him. "Name's Widow Neddles. Lives in that house there," he pointed. "Has a sink full of dirty dishes."

"You got that out of her, huh?" he smiled, "Guess we can close the case now!"

"I'm sure you'll get more," Chief Zimmer said.

"Captain will be here any second. She can wait."

Sheriff cruisers pointed spotlights on the victim and Widow Neddles screamed because dark blood pools turned to bright red. Living color. The arrow sticking out of the chest shined black, as Fran lay frozen, twisted in agony on his side. No one was near the boy. Deputy Smith made sure of it.

Dogs were starting to bark across the entire town, announcing that something bad had happened.

After Captain arrived and chatted with Widow Neddles, he released her.

She seemed to be getting better at saying she didn't know anything. "Do I have to pay for the phone call?" she asked over her shoulder to the Captain as Brighton walked her home. "What about my car?"

"It's safe inside the crime scene. The Deputies will bring it over soon enough."

"But I have some things in it. Could you help me carry them inside?"

"Deputies do all that. They were just talking about washing your dishes too."

"Oh that's so nice!" She beamed.

Dirty Dishes

He winked back.

"Make sure you thank them."

"Of course. You know I will!"

The Medical Examiner was the 17th cop to arrive at the scene. The IBO technician was flashing enough pictures to make a mosaic. Four investigators were flashlighting around.

"Ten to one the last person he talked to was Mutt." Detectives Smith and Weston said to Captain.

"Do it."

Smith nodded to Weston and they went to find Mutt. They joined Officer Brighton, already posted outside the boy's house. The three knocked and Mutt answered. They told him about Fran, standing in his doorway.

Brighton thought it was going to be his triumphal hour, but it wasn't that great.

Back at the crime scene, the K-9 unit had arrived in case the attacker fled on foot. The dog went right to the trash where Wendell had waited, but some old steak bones were around the area. "K-9's sniffing around the trash a lot," the handler said.

"Feed him lately?" Captain started grinning as he heard a steak bone snap. The dog tracked across the street. But after watching it go in circles and pee on something, both he and the Sheriff moved their attention to the Medical Examiner.

"Thanks for coming out. I wanted you to see it. Cut him up before the poisoned kid. The arrow is our best evidence," Captain said.

"It's a different modis?"

"We'll talk about MO's at the meeting."

"When will that be?"

"All day. All week all year! Clear your schedule. We don't have lives anymore. Have everything ready to display to the men at six. Can you do that?"

"All but the lab work," the M.E. said.

"Get on it." The M.E. walked towards the body. His young assistant tagged alongside.

"What are we gonna do?" the novice asked.

"First, we get to sharpen up some knives," the M.E. said.

12

Hordeland

Detectives Smith and Weston took Sid Mongrel, alias Mutt, in for questioning and started a series of worst experiences for the boy. At the Sheriff's Station, they de-boned him while his lawyer chewed gristle about next Friday's football game with Brighton behind the one-way glass.

Weston looked at Mutt. "Your lawyer buddy is right there, Mutt, so he can still hear if he wants too." Weston pointed to the mirror. "Of course your counsel is court appointed, so he's really on our team, so if you need to take a break, Mutt, you can ask him or us because we get paid by the same boss! You need some time?"

"How much time does Shoes have, Mutt?"

"Socks is clean out."

"You sure you don't prefer to be called, Sid?"

"What do you prefer, Mutt? Which one of your preferences got you four into this mess? What started the mess, Mutt?"

"What did you do?"

"How can we protect you if we don't know where to point our guns?"

"Who's pointing a weapon at you, Mutt?"

Weston turned to his partner. "Detective Smith? How about it? Would you rather get shot by a gun or an arrow?"

"A bullet any day!" Smith said. "Mutt, did you know our Kevlar won't stop an arrow?"

"How you going to stop one, Mutt?"

"First poison then arrow. Wow!"

"What's next, Mutt?"

"You upset some Indian Chief? Insult some Brave? Steal

some squaw?"

"Maybe it's a hunting arrow with a hunting tip! You ever seen a good broad head arrow tip, Mutt? They can cut you by just getting close!"

"What would all those razors do to you?"

"This killer's creative!"

"How's the killer going to kill you, Mutt?"

"You need to start thinking about things like that."

"Maybe a poisoned tipped arrow is next!"

"That'd fit. That'd be kind of cool, wouldn't it Mutt?"

"You ready for that?"

"The killer will use the same poison from Shoes and Socks and combine it with something else!"

"Maybe it'll be something special for you, Mutt?"

"Yea! I'll bet the killer's got something real special lined up for you! You're the leader after all. You're Mutt the leader!"

"Of course you led them right to the grave."

"Maybe he'll come up close and personal, Mutt. Just think! You'll see the killer just before you die!"

"Of course you won't be able to tell us then, will you? It'll be too late for all of us."

"He'll get away."

"You ready for that, Mutt? You ready to die knowing we will never catch the killer because your secret went with you into the grave?"

"Is it a comforting secret, Mutt? One that you want to sleep with for eternity?"

Mutt looked around. It wasn't going too good. Long ago he stopped answering and his lawyer had gone out for coffee again. Fear was changing his values, too. He was learning there were worse things than cops. That proved quite the shock. Cops around him kept looking over their shoulders and seemed to be there to protect him. He didn't buy their bluff, but he didn't want them to go away either.

A cop opened the door and handed Smith and Weston a file full of digital photographs just off the printer.

"These are full color pics, Mutt."

"Wow!"

"You should put these on your phone!"

Mutt saw Fran dead in a lake of blood and whipped his head away.

"Wait! These are better!" they held up a few of Shoes dead at the hospital.

Weston grabbed Mutt viciously by the scuff of the neck and half lifted him from his chair.

Mutt tried to push the photograph away but Weston was stronger and smeared the ink across the teenager's face.

"Now that one got wrecked, Mutt."

"Oh! Don't worry," he held up another of a glob that resembled Shoes. "This one is better!"

A starved, mangy dog circled far behind Dr. Carp's truck. It lumbered up in the blind spot, leaped onto the bed and snagged the fresh-killed opossum.

Caged animals freaked.

Spam turned and fired as the dog jumped, leaving an image of a bloodied head and a long marsupial tail sticking out both sides of a dog's mouth.

Carp pivoted and swung up his .45 pistol, but was too late. The dog and its reward leaped into the night and soon another fight enthralled as the opossum got shredded.

"The really starved ones always end up licking bullet holes for a while. I think that's the one who nearly got me the other day."

"Don't they run away from here?"

"Some, but here they get fresh meat and spring water on a schedule. Here, they're all dog!"

"How many?"

"Hard to tell. It's always pretty high around now. Winters really cut down the numbers."

"What about the cats?"

Carp smiled because headlights found the barn. "You'll need your gun here. Stay close!" Carp took up his .45.

"Why can't I have a big one?"

"They can't tell the difference in the dark. But right now they're all pretty starved and that makes any predator dangerous." The man got out with a light and growling was heard in the shadows.

Those tones were of starvation and they were desperate. They wanted food now! Dozens were near, but well hidden.

Carp swung the beam of light around, but none were close, they seemed to have been taught not to mess with the .45.

Spam kept bumping into the man.

"Relax, Spam. They ain't werewolves!"

Spam stayed real close. He knew the size of some animals Doc had supposedly euthanized over the years. And he also saw the gun out of the holster as the barn door was pushed along its runners and clipped to a contraption with a spring.

Spam couldn't see how it worked or what it did until they got back in the truck and drove inside. The tires then tripped something and the door closed behind them.

"It's good to have that door close quick," Carp said, covering the interior with his light and pistol.

Spam heard paws pounding earth outside.

Carp started a small generator and lights came on throughout the ancient barn.

Josh saw two quad runner 4X4's. One was nearly beat to

death, the other sparkled. "Wow!" Spam said.

"Good job with the library," Carp said, pulling deer carcasses off the truck. They hit the ground and dust and flumes of old hair puffed up. "You want the old one or the new one?" Carp asked as he hooked the deer feet together using short chains and a K-bar. As chain rattled the howling started. Claws scratched at the walls and turned Spam in a complete circle.

"I don't care," Spam said.

"I knew you'd say that," Carp said. "But stop gawking around. You're here because I need the help." The man knifed and threaded chain through holes pierced between bone and cordlike tendons above the back hoofs. Soon Doc had three groups of roadkill deer ready to be dragged. Six large coils of frazzled rope were dragged to the quads. He fed each end around its road kill grouping and brought all ends back to the quads and tied slipknots. With a yank he could release the flesh, drive on and save the rope for another day.

He adjusted the gun in his holster then went to Spam and they rigged the same feeding contraption to his quad. Carp slid the last two deer off the truck and onto the back racks of each quad and strapped them. He dragged the card board box of smaller roadkill critters to his front racks.

"Appetizers," Carp said.

"What do we do?" Spam yelled. By then a serious ruckus howl had started outside.

"Rule one is don't fall off your quad!" Carp said and showed Spam how to run the machine. The boy took a few glances around. The full canine frenzy climaxed when they warmed their engines. He saw the aged animals in their cages still on the back of the truck. Something was stirring in their souls that had never had moved before. They were hearing the howl of instinct. They had never known it was in them as they complained about Alpo and table scraps.

"What's going to happen to them?" Spam asked.

"We'll spring them after the feeding frenzy. It's their best chance."

"Whatta ya mean?"

"Let's just say they now live in a dog eat dog world!" Carp said. "Let's go! I try not to keep them waiting over a week."

"You mean . . ."

". . . It's a dog's life, Spam! Imagine that! You should know what that's like from Jr. High!" He was yelling over his engine, then he revved his throttle and pointed for Spam to turn his headlights on. The thumbs-up sign was shared and Carp tripped a spring and the doors opened.

Carp yelped them back with some pellet rounds, spinning a couple canines around. But overall, they seemed to know their hunger strike was over.

Each quad ripped out 100 feet of line, scattering the horde before their burdens grabbed and dropped their RPM's as their 800-pound loads gained momentum. Deer were soon dragging and bouncing after the ATV's at 25 mph, and even the smallest dog in the horde felt like a wolf.

Hundreds of dogs bounded in, diving fang first into dinner. As jaws locked, their bodies just lampreyed along until chunks broke loose. After a few miles of dragging and getting the various packs good and exercised, Carp released each pile of deer about 500 yards apart around the land. Each got swarmed.

Then Spam realized the crunching under his tires was bones.

Carp had been doing this for years. Decades.

After dumping, they coiled ropes in a stand of old forest. All was dark and calm. Engines were off, but they kept their head lamps on.

"What do you think?" Carp asked, panting.

Spam tried to catch breath.

Doc smiled and walked to a tree and took a line that had been tied to a branch. A deer skeleton, picked to the bone was lowered to the ground. Carp cut it off and tied a fresh carcass on from his ATV.

Spam saw Doc knee deep in white bones and deer hair, tying off rope ends to the quad and the deer. The middle of the rope looped up over a high branch.

Spam started doing the same with rope hanging on another tree. A lone meow fell down upon Spam. He looked up. Above them were cats, perched in the canopy. Out of the corner of his eye Spam saw a few small shaggy poodles.

"They're between worlds," Carp said. "They live on marrow." Carp checked the knots. They fired engines. Wheels dug in and hoisted the deer into the air until they were swinging pretty high up. The tree trunks had long been stripped of bark by claws. Carp shone light on the swinging deer. The carcasses were crawling as dozens of large cats, shredded through deer fur with claws and teeth.

Hair fell like snow.

Every branch beamed with glowing eyes of hungry, untrusting cats.

"Whoa!" Spam said. "Why don't they make any noise?"

"They're wild now," Carp said.

After hours of questions and answering and dodging photographs, the detectives had left Mutt alone, giving him an open door cell. But two hours later they woke him with the violent slam of a heavy metallic boom.

"Why you locking me down?" Mutt asked.

"Tommy just died." Weston spoke through the bars.

"Socks and Shoes have walked into the grave. And Fran ran into an arrow. Things are kind of getting worse aren't they?" Just then Detective Smith joined Weston.

"Since you're awake, Mutt, we should give you a chance to answer some more questions," Smith said. They yanked him back into the interrogation room along with his sleepy lawyer and started peppering him.

Strong. No fear. Ruthless and other related words were deleted from Sid's vocabulary that night, along with their meanings. He was the only one in the Dog Pound still alive.

13

Good Grief

In the predawn darkness of early Thursday morning, Superintendent Greenwood got his wake up call. Two of his students were dead from drug poisoning, probably murdered, and another, who was the friend of the poisoned, was murdered on a Tremble street. "So what we have here is... What do we have?" he asked.

"Well," Officer Brighten yawned into the receiver. "We're not that sure. It's not our show. Boys in brown bought it."

"You guys really want me to stay open? And put 600 panic-stricken kids in close proximity? And the killer may be one of my students! This is fertile soil for lawsuits."

"Naw, just activate the Crises Counselors. Kids are going to need that. We all will. And routine heals."

"Why are you telling me this? What about the killer? What if he kills a kid on school grounds?" Greenwood asked.

"Off the record, the killer is Mutt or whoever wants to kill Mutt, but can't because Mutt's in jail! So either way you're safe. Nearly the entire Sheriff's Department is on this. We all are. And we'll be all over the place. We'll wrap it up."

"If Sheriff and Chief put it in writing for me to stay open. I'm open. But who's gonna protect these kids today in case you're wrong?"

"I'm right. We'll be with you all day. Some detectives too. That good enough?"

"That'll do. But remember, kids are tense and parents are scared. Hey, Sheriff doesn't mind you boys being near the investigation?"

"It's our town, remember. They got their own style, but we

have the local knowledge."

Dr. Wienburger, M.E., walked into the cold, chemical preservative smelling morgue with two Krispy Kremes™ and a large cup of gas station cappuccino. It was 4 a.m.

The assistant had all three bodies out of the cooler and on tables. He had laid out stainless steel scissors, knives, saws and clippers. They were ready to cut.

"We haven't had three stiffs in this morgue since those visitors ditched and froze solid in the blizzard of '78!" He said and walked up to the table. On it was a boy with a black arrow sticking out of his upper chest. "We start with him. Toxicology won't be ready for today's round-up anyhow." He looked down at the boy who had been stripped naked and lay curled and twisted. The arrow had wrought his body in pain as if it had twisted tight all his ligaments like a fork spools spaghetti.

"Bow season start yet?" Wienburger asked.

"Nope. That's not until October 15th."

"Well, someone's mixed up."

"Think these are related? Since they're buddies and all?"

"Yup."

"How?"

"Well," he took a bite of donut and a sip of Joe, "that's what they're trying to tell us." Wienburger compressed his foam cup into Fran's stone froze hand and picked up a clipboard and clicked a pen. "Okay Dead Man, it's time to start talking!"

The assistant looked around.

Dr. Wienburger stared at him. "Judging by the fact more blood was on the road than in his body, what do you think happened?"

"He bled to death?" the assistant asked.

"But we just can't write that in our report now can we? What is the name of the artery that bled him?"

The assistant shrugged.

Wienburger twanged the arrow. "At least we know the angle of entry; we won't have to put a stick in him for that!"

Police Chief Zimmer was the only city cop invited to the Sheriff's Murder Meeting. That stuck in his crawl. Then he had to park a block away because the brown cars had taken all the good spots. Including the RESERVED FOR CHEIF spot. It was still dark but City Hall had become Murder Central. Gear flowed in as if they were moving in for good. Computers and desk bunnies settled the north wall. It was 6 a.m. Chief Zimmer's fear became real.

A Tremblen had tumbled and was now killing kids.

Chief remembered some infamous killers who had risen to haunt towns from some mighty common occupations. Mighty ordinary looking folks were sometimes the most horrible killers. A talkative, churchgoing man named BTK came to mind and Chief shuddered.

BTK was a Dog Catcher.

Chief knew apprehending a murderer at large could take years if the killer hunted at random. He also knew open cases ended careers. Open cases not only ruined families, they have been known to make ghost towns.

Window shades were down and City Hall business had been diverted to the library down the road. The City Planner had been crowded out and some children's field trips to the Fire Station next door had been cancelled.

Sheriff Harry was still in Lansing, soliciting FBI for help, but every other gun in the county seemed to be there. The boys in brown could sure produce manpower. And with a killer loose in Tremble, all resources were pooled.

Now that the Counties had come, pressure mounted. Without motive, they could only circle like buzzards above sand.

Chief had gotten the memo. The one that said if they didn't catch the killer in the first week, odds tripled in favor of the murderer to remain at large for six months. If they didn't apprehend the killer after six months, the odds were 50/50 that the investigation may take the better part of a decade.

Brighton handed over the private files to the Sheriff's team at 6:30 a.m. but he knew character profiles couldn't free Tremble from its fear. Brighton believed Chief. He knew those dogs crapped on someone's property who didn't want the cheap fertilizer.

Chief only wanted the short version of the dead boys' histories, so Officer Brighten's overviewed their academic files, disciplinary histories, at-risk behaviors, family backgrounds, short-comings, an the assortment of learning disorders and labels that seemed catalytic in uniting these children into what he called, 'Destructivites.'

"Just tell me what they did to get themselves killed!" Chief asked.

"I don't know."

"It's just paper without the event," Chief told Brighton before sending him back to high school like a parent. "Find the event. It's recent. Last week maybe. These are impulse killings. I don't think the killer's trying to make a statement, he's just trying to kill them dead and do it as quick as possible!"

Law Enforcement welcomed students into Tremble High School on Thursday morning. It was the second time in one week. Cops that were up all night ushered them in. Stories swirled up and over, down and around.

Students were sent to the gym bleachers for the emergency assembly. The bell had yet to ring and voices droned like bees cooling a hot hive.

The assembly took an hour to make sure everyone knew it was okay to feel and be emotional. A sympathetic woman ran the entire show and a strange calm was in the gym.

When it was done, four or five had to stay behind to yank tissues. A dozen called home, but most students just enjoyed being out of class.

Wendell did. He had a good day started. *Mutt's in jail! Three of the Dog Pound are dead! Two from my ivy one from my arrow! At least now I can face Deontra. But I must not finish Mutt until I find out who Bam Bam is!*

Throughout the morning classes, students went into Sherlock status. No one in any of Wendell's classes considered anyone but Mutt until one kid raised his hand.

"You wanna know something interesting about the killings?" a sophomore asked a teacher.

"You have it solved?" the teacher smiled to break tension.

"No! But they didn't take bad drugs. They didn't take Crystal Missal or something suicidal. And it's no 2nd degree accident. We're talking Murder One."

"Really? Mutt's in the tank for triple homicide?" teacher asked. "I can see that."

"I never said it was Mutt. Matter of fact, I know Mutt didn't do it."

"How?"

"To kill like that? Those murders took premeditation. You see Mutt as a premeditator? I mean seriously, he once came to school barefoot because he couldn't find his shoes."

Everyone spoke at once.

Wendell's teachers weren't inquisitive so far. Most were brainless machines who frowned at getting behind in their lesson plans because the standardized test were coming. He probably wouldn't be near a hot seat until late in the day with Mr. Thompson's gifted class that his parents had pushed him to take. If any teacher could sniff out a killer it was Thompson. If he survived Thompson it would go down in history as a miracle for sure.

So now, as students asked teachers about the killings, Wendell fought his urge to become an empty desk and started to straighten up and learn! *They're just rapist dogs. Oh, wait! I can't think like that!* He reminded himself and kept on studying. He memorized the ambiguity of student statements.

I still can't believe it!
Some farm kid from Eggville ate too many chickens.
Why would Mutt do that?

Wendell repeated common responses over and again in his head, sounding innocent, arrogant and confused. Hours passed. Wendell memorized. He could now say quite a few outloud.

"Mutt is mean enough to kill anyone!" Wendell told a person sitting next to him, but deep down, he knew cops would pop him like a fish egg three questions into any interrogation.

By 3rd hour, eeriness fell on campus like an eclipse. Then a surge zapped the student body when someone rumored school might get canceled for the week. The social order anthill got kicked. Teachers stood in doorways most of third and fourth hour, giving up on lesson plans and talking to co-workers. Some surfed the passion wave, teaching life lessons because death was in the air.

Deontra stayed out of discussions. She knew why they

were dead. They were dead because of what they had done to her. God had honored her whispers of vengeance. "Make them pay, God. Make them pay!" And like in Egypt, Death Angel Days had come to Tremble. But her prayers now haunted her. Guilt became awful. So, amid her crowded classroom, she closed out the whirlwind and focused her thoughts. *God, I forgive Mutt and his dead friends. I forgive them! And don't kill Mutt before he learns he's forgiven and that I won't rape him back.*

She finished and looked around, but all she saw were students more frightened than herself.

14

The Speak-Freak Mourners

Tremble High had a huge eating area, with a forty foot high ceiling and packed in all 600 teenagers in two back-to-back lunches. The place roared with stress. Nervousness exploded in sound as students talked a pitch above their friends and neighbors. All were arguing and most were nearly stoned on adrenaline. Seven cops stood sentry, bodyguard eyes roving the crowd for a possible killer. It was a great day!

Into this anxiety-enhanced mess walked Josh Spamp and someone threw a plastic bowl of chocolate pudding at him, erupting a table in laughter. Spam was again a de-stressor.

All who saw were reminded of Jr. High, and the prison of abuse Spam had endured. Those memories surfaced in most students and they felt an odd sense of comfort. It only took dark pudding on a white sweatshirt to spark nerves and connect all of the freshman and sophomores.

More turned and watched.

Conversation faded.

For in their past, either by commission or omission, they were all guilty of abusing Spam. Now in high school, Spam had just disappeared.

Until now.

They saw the chocolate spot on his white shirt and felt soothed. They remembered the comradely of cruelty and how they oppressed Spam to be weakest of all Hildago's caged monkeys at Tremble Junior High, where Spam was the one everybody could bite without getting bit back. And now students, frantic about a killer on the loose, regressed and chose comforts of tradition and prejudice.

Spam was again the sacrifice in which they stabbed, offering up their fears of inadequacy in return for a sense of normalcy.

But the manner and poise in how Spam had stopped, focused the teenagers. With part of his head shaved and stitched, this Spam had purpose, as if he was going to speak. He put his tray on a table and silence rippled through the room.

All hoped he would do something to take away stress.

"Are you gonna speak, Spam?" someone yelled from across the cafeteria. A short roar came like a burst, then backdrafted as all inhaled.

"Speak! Freak! Speak!" Someone yelled out and then it happened. Students rallied against death using Spam to scapegoat their fear. Like hippies in the 1960's hacking the Vietnam War, Tremble students sloganed Spam to protest murder.

"Speak! Freak! Speak!" All 241 chanted it. But no one in that cafeteria, really thought death could leave the air. Most just grooved to excite the moment.

Then Spam lifted one finger and all noise ceased.

Any second the bell would dismiss the group and upper classmen would invade.

A dozen seniors were outside the doors, waiting to eat and got vacuumed inside.

Three teachers, four counselors, Bounce the Lunch Lady and all seven cops looked at Spam.

The pudding-splattered boy inhaled; air seemed to disappear as everyone else took a breath, anticipating sound after seven years of silence.

It was imminent.

Spam's hand formed into a fist and he withdrew it to his chest. "Stanford Strings. Tommy Smith. And Fran Parkington are dead." His voice was strong and the student body was dumbfounded.

Death imminence crushed the area like rank of an Auschwitz furnace to a Holocaust denier and faces just withered.

Spam lifted three fingers up high. "Three are dead and you want to hear my voice? Yesterday they were alive. But today we laugh and search for jokes?" His voice elevated pitch. If he faked a punch the crowd would have flinched. If he said, boo, they would have jumped in their seats.

Spam commanded with authority. "Let us consider remorse! Come now to this corner and let us bend our knees in defiance of our distractions! Together, let us weep for our dead friends. Let us mourn to God for our dead hearts. Come."

The stillness was a microburst. No one twitched, but then as one organism, hundreds moved.

Spam took his fist from his chest and opened his fingers.

Students came hounded by doom, finality of death, and eternity. Peers gathered and held each other in utter silence.

Spam stepped up onto a table above the crowd and dropped, knees scattering food across trays.

All others knelt out of respect to a God of Judgement. To a God of reality who was but waiting to see them all the moment their own hearts stopped beating.

The release bell rang but it was like a soft alarm clock under a pillow.

Older students charged in, slowed to a walk, then stopped, awestruck. Many upperclassmen, who ventured closer to the sorrow, were pulled into solitude and stillness.

Death had become real at Tremble High on a Thursday afternoon.

The Speak-Freak Mourners

IBO photographs of the vics had been enlarged and now hung from whiteboards behind the small podium. They took away lunch appetite. Captain Campbell was briefing everyone on data processing and details. The meeting was now four hours strong and had no sign of ending.

"Good defense lawyers live for these cases. So we're going to do it right. We're not going to make a bottom feeder's career on this!" Captain said. The photos behind him captured the gruesome faces of the poisoned as well as the bloody clump of body tissue and black leather of the boy shot off his motorcycle. Many saw the murder weapon delivered and go behind the podium.

Captain Campbell rattled off notes from the Forensic Medical Examiner or M.E., then lifted the murder weapon.

Everyone sat up.

The Captain held out the long arrow wrapped in plastic. "Here we see what killed him." He flipped to a new photograph on his powerpoint, showing a similar, non-mangled, light green arrow tip. "It's a reinforced flat razor blade, about an inch and a half long with a separate razor inserted into its middle." He then held up a long brown arrow with blue and yellow feathers. On its tip was glued an identical arrowhead.

"It's called a Bear Broad Head and was manufactured only in light green throughout the 1970's and discontinued in the '80's because of screw on tips. This one here was on a display rack over at Shooter's Bows and Boots. There are hundreds of thousands of these around the country, but they're hard to find because serious hunters hang onto them. Many still prefer them to the new fangled stuff. This one appears to be about 31 years old." He pointed the similar Broad Head at the audience and they saw what looked like a "+" sign.

In the back row, behind Chief Zimmer, Detective Smith nudged his partner. "I bet that hurt!" Smith whispered.

Weston grunted.

"The bad news is Sid Mongrel, alias Mutt, didn't kill his friends. He's a dead end as a suspect. But we're pretty certain he's hiding something. Mutt doesn't know *who* killed his friends, but he knows *why*. It's something pretty incriminating because we haven't cracked him yet. Statistically, the top four angles are FFA, Felony Fire Arm, GTA or Grand Theft Auto, Possession or Trafficking of Narcotics or CSC. Criminal Sexual Conduct. We sent the murder weapon to the press. It's rare and we're in a small town so we're hoping for a break."

Murmurs rose throughout the room, making it seem like Mutt was the type capable of all four violations.

"But he's on his way to breaking," Captain said. "It's only been 18 hours. He's going home late tonight whether he wants to or not. Unless he gives up the goods. But we don't think he will tonight. We think if he does it'll send him to prison. Or worse. He's scared of something besides bars."

The mass of cafeteria mourners took on many shapes and tones. They quickly got the attention of the Crises Management Team, who rushed 15 members to strike while fire flamed.

Consolers moved in and out of the mob, rubbing shoulders and complimenting students on their grip, but nobody really saw them.

Students didn't engage in counseling. They just stared at the ground by their knees.

Not all teenagers were pulled in. Those used to having influence stayed at tables, ate their lunches and watched.

The epic gathering in the cafeteria stunned Jones Watson. Rarely do students get emotional. *Why are the little punks still here?* Watson looked around. He opened a big paper sack

The Speak-Freak Mourners

holding peanut butter, jam jars and bread and put them on the table. He didn't like the sorrow group crowding his space, but he was too stubborn to move and held his seat. One by one his mates ghosted in, sat and stared at the sniffling snots.

Watson figured the group to be over 200. He saw adults going from student to student but he knew they didn't belong. *Who could start such a gathering and why?* He wondered. Then he saw Ryan, one of his thieves, who was listening to a boy talking. Most circled that boy. *Why would Ryan be listening to a boy called Spam?* Watson's eyes lingered. One thing about Ryan, soft spoken and reserved, the boy was a thinking thief. He had a mean streak too. In a fight without rules, Watson would bet the farm on Ryan being king of the castle.

As Watson watched he relaxed for the first time. *Good job Ryan! Now I can get a full report!*

15
Match-Maker Mayhem

Pamela the cheerleading captain had buried the better half of her sensitivity in an unmarked grave nine years ago and burned the shovel. That ceremony suffocated the worst pain in Pamela Stanford's life. But when she watched the way students were showing sorrow in the lunchroom, a very disturbing memory popped up. Impossible! She had sunk it in the muck years ago, yet now it took a few breaths without permission!

The memory wasn't dead. It was alive!

She knifed at this new life in her. No decayed corpse of was going to come back to life as long as she was in control. *But it's breathing in me!* She shook her head. *Bam Bam is never coming back as long as I'm alive!*

Three dead. Who cares? But Mutt? My Mutt! She trusted him to stay quiet. Her eyes fired. *Someone is killing my kennel club! They are attacking me! Plan! Plan! Plan!*

All she needed now was to locate the target. Pamela eyed Deontra. The Cathaholic sat alone, not engaging the crowd gathered in the corner. *Good for you! So you want to protect how your precious little virtues got violated? Fine!* Pamela noted. *But who initiated the students to mourn?*

Fumbling adults were among them listening and playing the ever-sympathetic Oprah. But energy was fading and they were scurrying to keep synergy.

Pamela studied. *Where did the energy come from? Hmm. Who could command the student body to tears of sorrow for scum?* She watched the sufferers, collecting facts. In the next few minutes, she gleaned pieces of truth and then stammered, almost saying the name out loud. *Spam! The one who never talks? Is talking!*

Well Spam! Words echoed in Pamela's heart, *If anyone is going to lead students, it is going to be one of us!* She turned and ate her lunch, enjoying her friends as they degraded.

After the bell, Pamela dropped her tray and turned to leave, but Spam was standing in front of her.

Behind him was the exit door to the hallway. His hair was disheveled and he had a little shaved area where some black, blood-clotted stitches could be seen. His eyebrows were furry, like a rodent's, and his eyes seemed a little beady. A dull gray sadness came from them.

Thousands of words and phrases welled up inside Pamela, dark poisonous things, but she held them back until she could determine how or where to inflict her tongue.

Spam didn't move or turn. Nor did he care that he was staring at *Pamela Stanford*, Captain of the Cheerleaders!

This bothered her. Her stare was supposed to intimidate him. *Who do you think you are?* Her eyes drilled into him. *Did you forget the whole town knows you killed your brother by burning him in a gasoline fire?*

"Got a match?" Pamela asked. The words just flipped off her tongue like germs on a baby sneeze. It wasn't her style to destroy without a plan. To do so took away some reward. But the way her sound and fury entered Spam's ears, released venom and twisted his innards was *beautiful*.

His face contorted and she watched it do so with the fueled intensity of battle.

She fought the desire to give him her kiss of death as she watched him struggle to stand.

Then, he morphed before her into one who seemed wise to hardship. To one who knew the purpose of pain.

She cold smiled him. "You've come to the right person if

you want more," she said. "I'm pretty sure that I can hurt you more than your own parents."

The student body, shocked at Spam speaking, kept their distance from him for a few hours. They stepped aside in the hallways to let him walk by. But by last class, enough time had passed and it came up.

A teacher focused on him. Being primarily a senior level teacher, Mr. Thompson let this one sophomore class know everyday that they were beneath his senior status. It was almost like he believed it. He liked to peg students. It was a pride thing and Spam had just proven him wrong.

"So, Mr. Spam, you took it upon yourself to skip out of most of your last class by staying in the senior lunch? How do you justify that?" the teacher asked.

Everyone looked at Spam. Many knew Spam was better off if he took the fifth.

"I don't recall justifying it," Spam said.

"Did you learn not to justify decisions from your Vietnam friend?"

"I learn many things from many people. I learn many lessons from you."

"Good. Here's another. Ask your Dr. John Carp, killer of all the counties animals, how he got Dishonorably Discharged from the U.S. Military?"

"What's that?" a student asked.

The teacher went into great detail answering the question.

Spam looked at his worn shoes and wondered why Mr. Thompson was afraid of Carp. *Maybe Mr. Thompson was afraid that Carp was a murderer. Why would Mr. Thompson be afraid of a murderer? Does he feel he needs to be murdered?*

Seven of twenty-two starting football players and a bunch of scrubs sat out football practice that Thursday afternoon. They had joined the Sorrow Group; one determined to honor the dead until justice prevailed. To join the group, one had to give up something very important. It was kind of like lent.

Captain Ron Robertson could understand if his players were sitting out because they were afraid of getting killed or getting their parents killed. *But a Sorrow Group? Oh good grief!* It got worse. *Their sacrifice could go on for weeks?* Ron mulled this over and wondered how to tell coach. Ron didn't have too.

Some leaders of the Sorrow Group had explained to coach how their leaderless gathering (duh) wanted to respect the dead and give honor to how the murders were tearing apart Tremble.

Now it was coach's turn to figure it out. He called Ron in his office to help him understand.

"We can't punish them, though they're killing the team. They're killing us! Simply killing us! But," he grabbed Ron by the shirt and pulled him inside the circle of coach breath, "kids at Tremble don't all-of-a-sudden just start philosophi-sizing like this. Find who is behind it! If someone can influence the team to skip a practice, that someone can lead the team to boycott a Conference Game!"

"You serious?" Ron asked. Such evil was beyond his imagination.

"Dead serious," Coach said. "You want your scholarship and future to get stiff-armed by this, this Sorrow Group? You want to live with that the rest of your life?"

"No!" Ron said.

"Then see it as a big fumble drill and everybody is grabbing for the ball!"

"Where do I start?"

"By yanking kids off the dog pile and getting control of the ball. The good stuff is buried at the bottom! The leader is at the bottom of the pile!"

Captain Campbell looked at his watch after a deputy whispered to him during a five-minute break. He took a drink. His throat hurt from talking so much.

"You three." Captain pointed to ones with cold eyes off to his left. "Your team is up. Sic Mutt. Tear his pathetic life to pieces. Review Smith and Weston's notes then pressure that punk. Increase his misery exponentially until he goes insane or gives up the goods that will lead to the arrest. Sid's the focus point and the only one we got. Get the magnifying glass on him and align it with the sun. Scorch him until he cries for rain then crank the heat!" He paused, "And don't forget to keep the kid's worthless lawyer around in case someone competent pokes his nose in."

The three nodded. And behind their cold, lifeless eyes, they were scheming torture. They left and everyone sat.

"We got new case details on the victims." He opened yet another file.

Inside the Veterinarian Clinic, smells of innards and outtards stung Spam's nose. The boy's shirt was off and stench settled on his skin so thick it insulated him from the draft. His stooped shoulders rounded into a neck that seemed two vertebrae longer than normal. He turned his head and saw cats against the screen windows. They weren't fantasizing about free birds, they just wanted fresh air.

Spam didn't like how Agent Orange's eyes were looking at him. And that Rottwieller could stare. The dog couldn't stalk worth a flip because his wheel squeaked, but he could lock eyes with the best of them. Spam saw fresh poop smudged throughout the tire tread.

The veterinarian was running cold water over the pudding stain on his shirt. "So everybody just stopped and stared at you with pudding stuck to your shirt? What's that mean?" Carp asked.

"Just what it sounds like," Spam said.

Agent Orange hadn't blinked and was extending his neck a little farther than before. Loose skin folds on the outer edge of both nostrils were pulsing like little paddles, pulling him closer to a Spam sandwich.

"Agent Orange is giving me the creeps," Spam said.

"Watch out for him. He's been weird all day. He keeps eating the cat food and his guts are a mess. He's really stinking up the place. You noticed?" Carp smiled.

"Yup."

"And when their attention was on you, you broke your silence?" Doc asked.

"John? Why did Aslan's claw cut me so deep?" Spam asked, referring to a book Carp and him talk about where a kid gets his skin sliced off by a lion named Aslan.

"Do you think your wound is deeper than others?"

"I can't say, but I think so."

"You're probably right. But great love comes from hard suffering."

The boy pulled his knees under his arms and balled himself up. "I didn't tell you one thing."

"Oh?"

"I found the girl afterwards. She would have come looking for me, so I stepped in front of her and..." Spam was rocking now. His heels seemed to be setting the movement for his body, but then the man noticed the boy's feet were trying to *stop* the motion. Something was driving his young body more out of control. Carp dropped the shirt and came to steady his friend.

"She knew of Aslan's cut? She spoke of the fire?"

"She asked me if I had a match," Spam said he fell fetal then.

John caught him and guided him to the floor.

Spam's sobs resounded off the bloodstains on the tile as he laid in the stench and the horror of how he had killed his brother overpowered him.

Old Dr. Carp took a knee and rested a hand on the boy's shoulder. It had taken four years to re-sensitize Spam so he could externalize his internal mess.

Spam was becoming healthy and strong.

16

EPBM's

There's a killer on the road
His brain is squirming like a toad
Take a long holiday
Let your children play
If you give this man a ride
-sweet memory will die
Killer on the road
                -Jim Morrison

Under Tremble's streetlights, in restaurants and along sidewalks, all was still Thursday night. False fronted Ned's Bar had a slow gathering of old school, Tremble High grads talking glory days. No longer were they meaner or more cruel, however. They had become more civil. Back then, they had announced when and where they would face an enemy for a public battle. And for this, they seemed to share an air of gratitude as they drooled over beers.

Tremble as a city, blazed light on darkness. Electric meters hummed. Fathers strolled their porches and around their property perimeters; chatted with neighbors by mailboxes. Others families craved TV's blue glow and stayed behind locked doors as the latest local reports took their spin on the murders.

It had happened.

A murderer had come.

After so many years one had found his way into their city limits. Gun safes were unsealed. Weapons were dusted off and cleaned. Inside belts and behind doors, pistols and shotguns were loaded and tucked.

Canines became watchdogs. Sensing unrest like marmots before avalanches, they paced, waiting for reasons to bark. Their stone age survival tendencies whispered. It was time to earn their keep. It was time to guard.

State Police and extra cop cruisers from neighboring cities patrolled. They seemed to add strife by rolling slow on streets. Empty fields were spotlighted. The next step in safety was to bring in National Guard and Martial Law. One news show had mentioned that.

Little Angie Stone initiated EPBM at Reveered's house (Emergency Prayer and Bible Meeting). She called and spread the message to the faithful seven members of TBY or Tremble's Baptist Youth.

Angie's mom didn't like them meeting at Reveered's, but didn't have time to clean.

Angie Stone was short, barely 5'1", but what she lacked in height she made up in depth. She held hands with Jesus. Her primary Bible wasn't a cool, fashion-zone, neon teenager looking one; it was a big, dark leather thing that nearly doubled her weight. She had blond hair down to her shoulders and didn't wear makeup or jewelry. Not because her mom hated it or the church forbade it (which neither did in all fairness), but because she learned way back in Jr. High that it was just hype. Angie hated hype. She finished tying her boots, picked up her big Thompson Chain Reference Bible with the complete numerical system of chain references, analyses of books, outline studies of characters and unique charts, with pictorial maps and archaeological discoveries and left for Reveered's.

Small-boned, she was not a frail girl, and couldn't wait until Holy War tomorrow so she could get her hands on a gun and shoot Luke. Mr. James made him pay all right last week. But Luke's real Judgment Day was still coming and she wanted to be the one who squeezed the trigger that fired the grapes of wrath.

At Reveered's, all the teenagers were gathered around his old Ben Franklin wood stove in the big living room. Cast iron doors were folded open and blaze was throwing heat. Embers snapped from the fire once in a while and landed on shag carpet between charred spots. Near the stove, the chill of autumn was gone. They had been talking of murders and how school was freaked. They huddled closer than usual as if the murderer was in the darkness outside.

"So let me get this straight," Reveered said, "They don't know if the first two were murdered or just smoked poison?"

"What's the difference?" one girl asked, making Angie smile.

"Philip Morris thinks there's a big one!" Luke said.

"Then yesterday a kid named Fran something was murdered with a bow and arrow?" Reveered stayed focused. "Then at today's lunch someone picked on the boy who never talks, called Spam, and Spam started talking?"

"That's right," a boy said who no one really knew. He was invited at the last second by Luke. Tonight's group was bigger than usual. Kids who rarely attended church and weren't on Angie's call list had somehow gotten invited to EPBM. Over a dozen crowded the stove.

If there's one benefit to war, sports and natural catastrophe, it's how it unites the church, Reveered thought. Some names that Reveered was still matching to faces were Suzan Windstop, Wendell Shyly and Ryan Knack. Jill somebody was also there. She had just moved in from the Bible Belt and said she needed a church family.

Angie didn't like Suzan very much. Helen Keller could have sensed the tension between the saint and the sinner. As for Wendell and Ryan, Reveered knew their faces from church, but they hadn't yet been introduced. Ryan attended on Easter and Christmas with his family. And Wendell? His family seemed to come in late and bug out pretty quick.

"And then the silent boy talked?" Reveered asked.

"It was different, Reveered," Luke said. "Spam spoke. He connected, like he's been planning to grab us with those words for years!"

"And he's the one who lost his brother seven years ago?" Reveered asked.

"He's the one who caught his brother *on fire* and burned him up seven years ago," Angie clarified. "Not exactly something I'd want on *my* resume."

"So he knows the brokenness of life," Reveered said. "That would explain why he could influence like that. Boldness doesn't come without pain."

"He knows something all right!" Luke said. "He spoke amazing! We were, hundreds of us, and Spam just made us hear what he had to say and told us what we needed to do."

"Is there a chance it's what God had to say?" Reveered asked.

"But *you* don't even know what *he* said," Angie said.

"His voice was *way* weird. We *had* to listen to him!" Luke said.

"He said we should be mourning the dead. As if we didn't know that," Angie said.

"No. That's not all of it," Ryan said with some amount of presence. "He said our hearts were as dead as the murdered. I saw myself. It wasn't good."

"He made me feel dead. He caught me laughing at him. And I saw it too. It wasn't good," a tall kid said. He played the three big sports, football, basketball and baseball. He wasn't awesome in any of them but was always in the game.

Reveered nodded, deep in thought.

Angie Stone boiled. Normally, *she* led the discussions, and even though *she* had called the meeting, *she* had hardly got a word in. EPBM wasn't going as planned and the candy she had brought to stir responses was still in her purse. Her eyes narrowed in concern. *Nobody here knows anything about Spam except his miserable past; now he's being talked about with more respect than those who pray at the flag in front of the whole school! Everything about this situation is wrong!*

"What do you think, Angie?" Reveered asked.

The girl paused, clutching her Bible and milking light. But she couldn't find the right words. "I don't know," she said.

"What do you mean?"

"Offer her some candy, Reveered." Luke said. "That'll get her talking."

The man ignored Luke and stayed with Angie. "Do you think the power of God moved in your school today through the boy called Spam? It sounds like a lot of kids got moved out of their comfort zone."

"I don't know. I don't think so."

"You gotta be kidding me!" Luke said. "You're telling me I didn't feel guilt?"

"I did," said another girl named Susan.

Angie looked at her and nodded. She knew Susan had countless good reasons to feel ashamed.

"I felt guilt too," said the curly blond haired boy, named Wendell.

"Can such corporate guilt come outside of God?" Reveered asked and looked at Angie, but she had her head down.

Angie stayed still and quiet, not hearing the others. After a while her eyes came up and she looked around. But inside, her self-talk kept whispering. *I'll have to go with mother and talk to the Deacons. Mr. James, AKA Reveered, might not be qualified to lead a Bible Study if he allows everyone to spend this much time talking about a boy and not the Bible. I could have left my study notes at home and no one would have known or even cared!*

She pulled her pinched finger from where it marked a verse in her Bible and closed the book. She raised her hand patiently until she was called on. Then waited until everyone looked.

"I feel that we should cancel Holy War out of respect for the dead," she said. "It's cancelled for tomorrow."

Jones Watson's friends invaded his house. His crooks always hung out anyway, if they changed now it might look suspicious. Watson didn't know what to do. But they all looked at him so he took Pamela's advice. After all, she was like him, a leader and he was honored that she had cared enough to track him down and share some of her fears as well as give advice out of mutual respect. Plus, on simpler terms, it always felt good when a pretty girl talked to you.

"Who cares?" Watson relayed her message to his team. His words fell flat and sounded good. "Mutt and his dogs never done nothing to us or for us. After all, we all got it coming!" He laughed now, breaking tension. "I just hope that when it's my time to go, someone doesn't arch me with a black arrow and watch me bleed like road kill!"

They laughed, especially Ace Dingle. He had earned his keep after dancing with Maybell King. "Kids at my last school in California bought it sometimes," Ace said. "It's supposed to happen. Tremble's a real school now!"

Faces nodded.

Watson looked around the room and frowned.

Ryan still hadn't shown up.

Around town other groups met. Ron Robertson guided his huddle, and like Pamela wanted, he rallied that Tremble had made it to the next level. "What doesn't kill us, only makes us stronger!" Ron said. "And for tomorrow's game, we need all the strength we can get!"

"Bring it on!" a player toasted. "May the killer keep killing! May we keep winning!"

A half-mile away Pamela led her squad which was unofficially called, The Beautiful People. She broke routine, stemming compliments, to discuss mortality.

"It's growing pains. We're in the cycle all schools go through. Let's just hope it doesn't happen once a month!" She said this and they giggled. And then they came to her and bought some stuff to help them. Pamela frowned at this and hoped Ron and the others were doing better. If her numbers stayed this bad, they wouldn't be able to do Cancun Two for Spring Break.

Reveered looked at Angie Stone, then at the others around his sagging, old wood burner, then turned back at Angie.

"Angie, I'm officially uncancelling the Holy War you cancelled," he said.

"It looks *real* bad right now in light of the killings," Angie said. "It looks real bad and I'm worried about our image."

"People say I'm strange, but that doesn't make me a stranger?"

"People are dying for real, Reveered!" she looked at group. "It's not a game anymore."

"We don't call it Holy Game. It's Holy War because war is the only constant between good and evil."

"Then, I for one, will boycott. I gotta go, Reveered. If you change your mind, call me quick. I may be doing an alternative activity."

"What if a Holy War is upon Tremble High right now,

Angie?" he said. Faces in the group moved in unison as if at a tennis match.

"How?" Angie stood and looked down at those seated. "Those boys who where murdered weren't no angels. They were the Dog Pound. I still think its best to just gather at the church to pray," Angie said.

"But wouldn't that be doing what Spam suggested at lunch? To pray for the heart of the school?" Luke asked.

"Is it?" Angie asked.

"Yes."

"Then maybe I'll need to think of something else."

"I challenge your motive, Angie. I really do," Reveered said.

"What's my motive have to do with anything?"

"Motive is everything," Reveered said. "Why don't you come back tomorrow? Boycott Holy War by staying at the fire. Keep it burning. More are coming than ever and they'll need your passion for God."

"Let me think about it. I'm not sure I understand what you want," she said and got up and walked out the door.

17

Cages & Crimes

Released from the cop shop on Thursday night, Mutt was driven home and sat with his drunk mother at the kitchen table. But home wasn't where his heart was.

Cops had cannibalized his ticker.

Mutt shifted to his left to see around the gallonish shaped yellow bottle of $3.99 wine, which stood in front of his mom. He knew she was in bad form because she didn't offer him a drink.

There was a burnt plastic smell throughout the house because a smoldering lamp was stuck into the TV. News had disrespected her Sid. *And where's my loser ex?* she thought. *Still on the run!*

Mutt didn't know if he could answer if his mom was in a talking mood.

Cop Q&A had crushed his thinking.

Cops had caught him in more lies than he thought he had ever told. It took hours to convince them he didn't kill Fran. Then after a few hours on Shoes and Strings, he nearly confessed up his long list of dirt just to get relief.

That scared him to take The Fifth and he shut his mouth. But his silence didn't stop the cops.

Detectives pounded his ears in stereo with thousands of questions. Grilling him on how he poisoned and shot his friends dead. It took hours, days, years!

Now his brain was but an ocean-stink-piece of sponge, and Mutt hated the only thought the cops had let him own. The thought now echoed. *You'll never sleep until you're free!*

Cops had said that about a ca-zillion times. They put it in

is long-term memory. They also convinced him that he might not have that long to live. "Don't get comfortable at home, Mutt," one had cautioned again as others stacked notes into piles. "Maybe it's *your* death day!"

"You'll never be free from us until you're free of the murderer. If he doesn't get you tonight, we're bringing you back tomorrow and the next day and the next. Then we'll start putting the type of pressure that makes you long for prison!"

"How about it, Mutt? Is tomorrow your day? Is tomorrow the *Day of the Dog*?"

Mutt thought Smith and Weston were bad, but then the three Gestapo types attacked him hard. They had beat him down like an Aryan Nation loudmouth in an all-black prison.

Mutt now looked up and saw his mom and wondered if he looked as bad as her.

Cops had made him long for his cell over this home. But all Mutt could hear, even at the table with his mom, was the cops.

"The one who murdered Fran is looking for you Mutt!" Cop voices echoed.

"What did you do?"

"Who did you piss off?"

"How many arrows does he have?"

"Do you know how cheap an arrow is, Mutt, we're talking cheap! And they're everywhere!"

"Have you ever been shot by an arrow, Mutt? You know how many razor blades are on the point of a broad head?"

"Who's hunting you, Mutt? Who's stalking you?"

"We can't help you until you help us."

"We can't protect you until we know what you did."

"What did you do, Mutt?"

"You take money from The Man?"

"What's his name, Mutt? We know there's The Man, Mutt.

We'll catch him too."

"He knows you're with us now, doesn't he? That's why he can't get you a descent lawyer, isn't it? A good lawyer would keep us away from you but the Man can't do that can he? He knows we could trace his money from the lawyer back to him, doesn't he? Doesn't he Mutt?"

"He knows you're rat'n him out. He knows you're messing with his drug money, Mutt!"

"Did he poison Shoes and Socks and murder Fran because of something you did?"

"Tell us what you did, Mutt."

"What did you do, Mutt?"

"The killer's looking for you, Mutt. Only he won't be nice like us. He'll be mean, Mutt. Real mean."

"You're the Top Dog, Mutt! He's going be extra evil with you!"

"What'd you do, Mutt?"

"Tell us what you did and be free."

Then the cops changed tactics.

"You know Fran's cold dead body is on our metal table in the morgue at the back of our slammer? Right on the other side of this wall!" He slapped the brick. One got up and opened the door.

"You want to go see him? Think you would recognize him now? The M.E. has cut him into pieces for bite-size evidence?"

"Think you can put him back together?"

"You believe in Jesus, Mutt? I wonder if Jesus could put Fran back together again? He brought Lazarus back from the dead after being gone for a few days, but it must be different for a person whose been *disemboweled*! Don't you think?"

"You should see what the M.E. did to Socks and Shoes! You'd think he had used a chainsaw!"

"Time for bed, Mutt? You ever sleep on cold metal, Mutt?"

Cops had even woken him at 3:30 a.m. and told him Socks and Shoes had joined Fran in Morguetown.

"You want to come over and take a look?"

"You want to ID them for us, Mutt? They're your friends, not ours. Maybe we got the wrong kids in the butcher building?"

They left and maybe Mutt slept for an hour.

Then the cops came back for breakfast. They carried in steaming hot egg and sausage sandwiches and gave Mutt a cold, crusty cinnamon Pop Tart™ and started asking him the same questions all over as if they had them written down.

Now Mutt shuddered as he remembered. He shook his head as he looked at his mom. But still the cop questions lingered.

"They're all cut open now. It took hours, Mutt."

"They're chainsawed."

"We should have put you in with the M.E. when he delved into their stomachs and squeezed out their intestines to see what they had for breakfast."

"Are they your friends, Mutt? Or is this what you do to your enemies? Talk to us Mutt."

"How's your breakfast, Mutt? We gave you that because that's what Socks had for breakfast. A good old Poptart™! Strawberry."

"Is that water we gave you too warm?"

"Did you know there's over 40 feet of intestines, Mutt? Maybe the M.E. will ask us to give him a hand in the squeezing of your guts. We might have to squeeze you tomorrow Mutt. Eat up Mutt so then we'll know what you ate! Do it to help us out a little?"

"Tired, Mutt? What did you four do to wake up Hell, Mutt?"

"We'll find out no matter what. You can tell us now or the M.E. will cut you open or pull an arrow out of your chest."

"He'll squeeze out your guts, Mutt."

"What did you eat yesterday?"

"Maybe the killer has something special planned for you, Mutt? You are the leader of the pack, you know?"

"Leaders always get something extra special! What are you going to get, Mutt?"

"You don't need to tell me what you had for breakfast yesterday, Mutt. We'll find out soon won't we?"

"What did you do, Mutt?"

"We can't protect you until you help us."

"He's coming for you, Mutt."

"Is the killer really mad or is he just crazy?"

"How do you protect yourself from someone who is insane, Mutt?"

"He's obsessed, you know that, right? He's obsessed in killing you! He's already seen himself kill you a thousand times in his twisted, sick mind! Why does he like it, Mutt? Why does the sicko enjoy fantasizing about killing you? Only he's ready to do it for real now!"

"Are you ready to die for real, Mutt?"

"A couple of days, Mutt. Killing sprees always end in a couple of days."

"How's the assassin going to kill you, Mutt?"

"Is your little secret worth dying for?"

"The good news is that when he kills you we'll catch him and make the arrest! Case closed and we go home and sleep! We'll be heroes! But you? Oh, that's right! You'll just be dead! And you know what? People will be so thankful we got the killer that they won't even care about you. Poor old Mutt. Kind of like Old Yeller. Tremble will get the new puppy and will just forget about Old Mutt!"

Mutt had a bad day with Sheriff detectives. Now he was having a bad evening with his mom. Something about the lamp in the TV made everything horrible. The killer must have seen him on Fran's bike moments before.

I was in his sights! Mutt turned his head as he tried to swallow. His mom poured herself another drink and shoved bottle toward him. It glided across tabletop.

He stopped it. He unscrewed the cap and took a good chug and wiped his mouth with the hand that held the bottle.

Investigators Smith and Weston were posted in a cruiser outside.

Mutt turned and looked out the window at them. *They're here to protect me!* It didn't make him feel any safer. He knew they hated him. They wanted him dead more than the killer because he had wasted so much of their time.

Mutt blinked. He had seen a doctor scalpel apart eyelids of his friends to keep poison flowing. *How can I protect myself against a person who did that?*

Mutt left the kitchen silence and went upstairs and pushed the dresser in front of the door then threw off his covers as if there were scorpions on the bed. Mutt didn't know what the killer was planning; he just knew the killer was *premeditating*. He knew wasn't going to go to sleep and find out.

His court appointed lawyer was pathetic.

The county boys had hamburgered him.

The lawyer's D- college training failed him and he was sweating like an Inuit with the Aztecs when he tried to get between Mutt and the cops.

Why don't I have a better lawyer? Why doesn't my father help? He shook off the thought. Toughness doesn't come from being protected by some suit. But deep down Mutt knew he was lucky to leave without linking the murders to Deontra.

Now he wasn't so sure if it was luck.

That's it then! That's when it all started! That stupid Catholic girl. And we never even got her good.

He looked out the window and shivered. *Where is the monster? How can one little cop car keep it away? Is it already in my house? Is he watching me now as I look out the window?*

Mutt stepped back and closed the curtains after seeing dozens of places where a sniper could be perched.

As Thursday faded out, La-Z-boys® captured Spam and Carp and no cats were in the clinic. It had the makings of a pretty good night.

"If I told you once," Carp said, "You have to add the A&W® first. That way you don't fizz out the pop."

Spam scooped foam and ate it. "But the ice-cream is supposed to fizz out the pop. That way you don't fart all night."

"Really?" The man pondered the connection, then went out to the kitchen and dumped his root beer float in a dog dish for Mrs. Tinkerton's St. Bernard. "Hey!" Carp yelled as he fixed his second float using Spam's technique. "Tell me about this girl."

"The mean one?"

"Yeah!" Carp said, and returned with someone's poodle running alongside, trying to catch rootbeer float runoff. Carp sat, levered his feet and the small dog jumped by his feet too. He grabbed the launch lever and cranked it down and up, flinging the over-friendly poodle off toward the TV. "How bad off is she?"

"She hates."

"You never talked of her before. How come?"

"She scares me. She out-meaned her Jr. High nick name, Bam Bam."

"Really? Hard to out-mean a name."

"You think I'll ever outgrow Spam?"

"No. Tell me about her."

"She's just mean and cold. Cold like space."

"She evil?"

"I don't know. I think she's hateful."

"Why?"

"I don't know. Maybe she's been hurt. Hurt like me. But is it possible?"

"Trust me," Carp said. "If rage is her life, she ain't got no life. Rage eats everything. You included if you're not careful."

"Really?"

"Rage from hurt is a black hole. Imploded star! A bowling ball of mass with the weight of a million planets! It makes you crave to be offended, which you hate, so you have an endless energy supply to power up your victim planet forever."

"Can she be helped?"

"Of course."

"How?" Spam asked.

"God and prayer. Anyone who helps define her hate will become a target. At least that's what I've done to people, you know, I mean people who showed me stuff about myself never really got off the hook. To expose hate is to put yourself in harms way."

"So if she sees Aslan's claw, she'll try to tear apart Aslan?"

"No. Cause He's Aslan. But if you try, she'll attack you and trust me Spam, you ain't no Aslan!"

"I'm going to get creamed."

"Always will. Son of God. Servant of God. Soldier of God. You grew up fast. You know the purpose of warrior pain. And it has made your theology anti-culture. Anti-comfort!"

"That's good, right?"

"Heck yes. All cultures waiting for the Messiah never

pegged Jesus. To see God one has to go against culture."

"Why's America see pain as bad?"

"Never underestimate the power of stupid people in large groups."

"You mean sheople?"

"I never said that and I ain't gonna hack on the church. I'm nearing the end of my 20-year-plan. You just go to school and gut it out. School's just a bunch of brainwashing crap anyways. The silver lining is that you get hurt a lot, and God works through pain."

"What of *her*?"

"What *of* her?"

"What if she comes for me?"

"What if you go to her? Maybe that's better. Go to her and maybe be the sacrifice that's too dumb to die. Or maybe it's true that inside every mean girl is a nice one waiting to come out."

"Isn't that Vietnam Charlie theology?" Spam asked.

"Don't fight dirty with *me*."

"Why did you get Dishonorably Discharged from the Military?"

"Where'd you hear that from?"

"One of my teachers."

"Gene Thompson?"

"Yes. How'd you know?" Spam asked.

"You'd be surprised what I know about Gene Thompson. So would Gene for that matter. But you know that answer. I was discharged because I killed soldiers, Spam. I am a murderer."

"But you were in Vietnam! You were at war!"

"That's one way to look at it."

18
Birds & Obits

School started Friday morning like an unplugged diesel engine in arctic cold. One in four students was gone. Flags were at half mast and a hard frost had come, making uncut grass look silver.

Spam didn't know what the day would bring. His Veterinarian shrink didn't talk much after being asked about war crimes. Carp only repeated two truths.

"Keep standing. Keep speaking."

Spam now wondered if he was ready for the evolution, but Carp had always said it would come.

A dozen students were waiting for Spam as he entered the main doors of the school. They joined him as he walked to his locker.

"Sheriff guys came to my house last night," a boy said. "What is going to happen?"

Spam stopped, causing a slight pile up. He met the boy's eyes. "If good students do nothing, evil can do whatever it wants to!"

As if the boy was a bird at a feeder, he took the chunk of truth and flew off.

Three girls came alongside. "Do you plan to help solve this mystery?" They were passing the library. Only it had a different purpose today.

Dozens of sheriff detectives were herding parents into groups. Mass investigations were brewing at Tremble High.

Spam pointed. "Mystery isn't an unsolved murder. Mystery is the coexistence of good and evil."

"What's that?"

"It's a fight to the death."

"Here at Tremble High?"

"No. Between God and the Devil. But the field of battle is the human heart."

"Who killed those boys?"

"One who lost the battle in his or her heart. God said, 'Cain! Evil is crouching at the door of your heart and you must master it!'"

"What happened?"

Spam looked at her. "Cain murdered his brother. Then and now."

Many stayed quiet after that and just walked with Spam. It wasn't obvious. He wasn't leading rats out of a city with a flute.

But senses of all students were aroused and keenly aware of a new peer group forming. Whispers and stares followed Spam like they did back in his days of death. As Spam dialed his locker the first bell rang.

A senior girl asked, "you spoke with authority yesterday. How do you learn that?"

"I don't know. Authority is a rare voice for me. I'm tempted to take the brand of beast with every breath." Spam opened the locker and a newspaper clipping fell to his feet. He bent down and picked up the press release of his younger brother's obituary. He turned his cheek to better face this razor-bladed slap. Then he faced them and read the news article to the group. A minute later, he handed it to a tall girl, who took it and showed another.

"Someone wants to remind me of my history," Spam said. "And how it doesn't appear to point to a good and perfect God." He closed his locker door.

They watched.

A half-dozen were still reading. When they felt him looking at them they stopped and saw his sadness.

"That's why," Spam nodded at the news piece, "When we start our search for God, we must look beyond our history. Our comfort is always secondary to the building of God's Kingdom." Spam left them there, hovering over the news clipping. He wondered how it would be when he met the person who was cruel enough to unbury the achieves and deliver the article.

"Is that why you never talked? Were you running from this?" Someone called out, waving the article.

Spam stopped and turned. "People avoid God by becoming busy and distracted. I embraced neither of those evils."

The bell rang and halls emptied. The principal came on closed circuit television and Murder News suckled every student to the inline feed. He made a few housekeeping comments, then talked about football. "We need, *everybody,* to come out and support Tremble's first ever undefeated football team this late in the season. We are making school history! And we expect the whole to unify and play!"

Divided throughout the classes of the school, the growing group of boycotting athletes squirmed.

Then the principal introduced Captain Campbell of the County Sheriff who had been seated next to him.

In his classroom, Wendell adjusted his long sleeved shirt and rested his right arm on his desk. Duct tapped around his thick forearm muscle below his elbow was a half an arrow and its tip. Beneath his shirt cuff, along his wrist waited the flat, razor-bladed, broad head tip. Wendell had removed the perpendicular center razor so he wouldn't slit his own wrist. With a simple adjustment, he could slide the arrow down so its point would extend to his fingertips. He could insert the butt of the shaft into another slit in thick tape around the middle of his forearm. Soon he would ambush Mutt, up close and personal and right in the neck! He knew bloodshed would drench him, but Deontra deserved the best execution he could imagine.

Captain Campbell leaned forward toward the microphone. "Tremble High School is safe and a full investigative force is on campus as well as four city police officers. Your security is primary to us and you have nothing to worry about."

Wendell looked around and nodded. It was good not to worry.

The detective lifted some pages of notes. "Currently, we are pursuing many leads in the triple homicide of your school mates. We are going to be speaking with many of you today even though the murders happened off school grounds and are likely unrelated to anything on your campus. We plan to speak with everybody. Naturally, any student who has knowledge of any activity they think is related to the homicides is to come to the library where we will be conducting interviews with over 100 students chosen by lottery. Those selected are only answering routine questions." The speaker paused. "Parents have already been gathered."

"I encourage all of you to be cautious in what you say. A homicide is upon the City of Tremble. Withholding information could produce a felony charge and can lead to your arrest. If you have insights that will advance our investigation, come to the library as soon as I conclude or call Silent Observer." He held up a number.

"You have the right to deny our questions on grounds that you are without your legal counsel. We are providing court appointed counsel to oversee each interview and your parents have been called in because time is of essence. But, if you chose to deny an interview, a separate task force will escort you to Head Quarters along with one or both of your legal guardians, so you can speak to us in the presence of your legal counsel. As always, if you feel in danger, report suspicions to any law enforcement agent."

Men with proper ID's filled hallways. Most were off-duty cops, firemen and EMT workers.

Tremble cross-trained.

Students looked around, adjusting to the escort invasion and a whole new routine.

Knuckles rapping on hard wood doors started their day.

Inside English Composition, Pamela sat next to her friend, Sherri.

"What did Spam do when he saw it?" Pamela's eyes brightened with excitement. Both girls paused as an adult fetched another student to be taken to an interview station.

Sherri didn't want to answer, but Pamela pushed.

"You so much have to tell me. What was his face like when he picked it up?"

"He was hurt," Sherri replied.

"And?"

"He read it to his little crowd." Words slapped Pamela's face red.

"Outloud?"

Sherri nodded and looked away, knowing bad news for Pamela was bad for her. Next time she would lie. She didn't know why she told Pamela the truth to begin with. Except, somehow, it just seemed that what had happened in Spam's eyes was worthy of being told and re-told. Sheri watched Pamela reach into a purse and pull out two more news clippings.

"Which one should be next? His mother's obituary or his father's?" Pamela asked.

Sherri just looked at them.

Pamela pulled one closer.

"Let's use his mother's and stay chronological," Pamela said. She rose and approached the teacher and told him she needed the hall pass. He was a guy teacher. They never asked her for a reason.

Cops made Mutt wear a wire, but worse than that, they changed his thinking.

Old Mutt, pig-hater and anarchist, was fading instead of burning out. Now he saw his wire as a way to stay safe. He was a safety boy, a mere step from being a piglet.

"Did being a dog help you become a rat?" Smith asked.

Mutt looked around, nervous from hallway traffic. He felt the tape pull at an island of skin where they shaved a bald spot on his chest.

Ear-pieced deputies were in front and behind.

Mutt felt like a piece of bait and knew his predator days had ended. He didn't like being prey and his eyes, facing frontward, felt oddly out of place. He turned both ways a lot and even looked behind every few steps. Fear started a manufacturing company in his heart as he got ready to walk the hallway.

"Just be normal," Detective Weston said. "Pee in corners. Lick you butt. Stuff like that! It's not very likely the killer will try for you with us around. But who knows? You were the leader, and killers like to make public statements!" He drew his side arm, checked the safety and holstered it.

"Remember Mutt, most murderers want to get caught," Smith added. "They have this inner battle thing going on inside their kill-hungry brain, and some are really, really driven! Are you sure you don't want to tell us what you did, Mutt? It might be your last chance."

Mutt forced himself to stay quiet. *A killer who wants to get caught?* Mutt's mind garbled. Mutt was no criminologist, but he knew that didn't sound too good. *It was one thing to have someone hate me and try to kill me, but now someone was willing to die to kill me!*

"Nothing to say to us, Mutt? Amazing!" Weston said. "Quite rare to have a suicidal sociopath eager to make the ultimate sacrifice just so he can expose one of your nasties and yet you say nothing. Your law-dodging-Wanted-father been teaching you? How 'bout your ma? Tipping bottles sounds passive. You speak to us boy and you can still survive this!"

Mutt closed his eyes.

"Don't worry about us, Mutt, okay? We're wearing Kevlar. We're on top of our game and have enough bullets to invade Poland. But of course, he's not after us is he? Not that we'd fire our guns anyway. You can't expect us to fire our guns in a crowded hallway to protect you, can ya? We might hit an innocent by-stander. People will care! We'd get a few months of no-pay so we're not going to risk it. But if you're killed because we don't fire? We'll just be heroes because we flushed out the killer! And you? Oh! You'll just be dead. Sucks to be you, doesn't it, Mutt?"

"How about it, Mutt. Anything to say?"

Mutt looked at them with empty eyes. *I should have never touched that Catholic girl. God is on her side.* Then he blinked. *Some God...letting one of his daises get ganged!* But his inner smile didn't stay long as the cops opened the door, activated the wire and shoved him into the stream of bodies in the hallway. It was between bells.

A twinge of something heavy had sunk deep in Mutt's stomach like cold lead. He never felt anything like it before and it was fertilizing paranoia.

Birds & Obits

Cops nudged him into traffic and he was paraded down a hallway. Cops before him. Cops behind. No turning back. He walked the endless plank.

Mutt saw Deontra pass him and she met his scared eyes. Mutt stopped, his blood rushed to his head and he went dizzy with fear. As she passed, he stopped stone still in the middle of the crowded hallway. Dozens of students paused and just stared at him, amazed to see him in school. Mutt grabbed the wire. "Help me!" he called out.

The cops charged in and circled him only to see he wasn't in danger. He might have been dying of an anxiety attack, but they weren't too concerned about that.

Students saw the sting operation go bad and wondered how Mutt could sink so fast.

Guilt had always been a foreign substance to Mutt, something that got shoed away like a fly on a cheeseburger. Now remorse had come into his body like a virus, and it found fertile territory because his life, fire-bent on anarchy had never made antibodies to fight shame. Now it was in him like Ebola, and he had no defense mechanisms to stop guilt from infecting his mind.

19
Breaking Bad

Deputies Smith and Weston walked up and looked down at the hyperventilating Mutt who was now sitting on his haunches against some lockers. They waited as waves of rubber-necking students passed by, then they put their hands to Mutt's shoulders and yanked him up.

"Get up Mutt, you're acting like you're walking The Green Mile! Get a grip!" They took him back into traffic flow, brushing aside students until they reached the office area by the three pairs of double doors at the school's main entrance. Once there, they met the three Gestapo-type interrogators. "You guys have a paper bag or something for Mutt?" Weston asked. "He has stress."

"No," one said.

Another pointed at Mutt.

"We've been looking for you, Mutt. You have to come with us. We got big questions now."

Mutt's lawyer was with them and held up his hands apologetically.

Mutt's heart faltered.

The third cop drew an index finger across his neck, motioning for Weston to radio back and get the tech to disconnect Mutt's microphone.

Weston did and gave them the thumbs up.

They took Mutt against the crowd for a moment and reached the exit. "Get used to the short leash, Mutt. It's that or a pine box."

"Ever slept in a pine box, Mutt. The one about the size of a coffin?" one asked as Mutt pulled off the tapped wire despite onlookers.

The three interrogators marched him outside. It was still between bells.

Many students just stopped and looked at Mutt. *The catchers caught the Mutt doing something!*

Others thought, *They're arresting him! He's the killer!*

Wendell Shyly didn't think either. He leaned against lockers and hooked his thumbs back on his pockets, burying the broad head against his jeans. *That was close.* But there was a part of him that still thought he could have done it. He fingered the razor now and felt its power.

Deontra saw Mutt leave too. Like Wendell, she now watched Mutt get led into a squad car. Her fingers touched the cold, wire-meshed glass in the door as cops drove Mutt away. The outside sky was gray and hallway lights buzzed and students cleared away, prodded by the pending tardy bell. Outside looked cold. Inside felt stale. The air was bad in both places.

She turned and saw a boy watching. *Is he watching Mutt or me?* She looked at the clock. *I gotta go! Run!* She paused, then walked toward him unafraid. *I'm the only person who knows God's Death Angel is here! And I'm the only one who knows why,* she said to herself. She came closer to the boy. *I will not fear.*

He had not turned away from her but stood still in the emptying hallway oddly looking at her.

She walked to him. "What is your name?"

"Wendell."

Her voice faulted. She wanted to say more but knew her voice would crack and reveal shame. She lowered her eyes, but noticed he was not gawking at her.

His eyes were kind, but frightened. Maybe more frightened than hers.

She lifted her gaze and met his eyes and it didn't bother her that she had to blink away a tear.

"And your name is Deontra."

She wore white. Her face always looked richer and darker in white. Her dark, deep eyes shown out from under perfect eyebrows and her cheekbones showed strength and courage. All her hair flowed back, some bunching on her shoulders but most running down the middle of her back.

"How do you know that? I mean, how do you know my name?" She looked at him and saw him struggling as if he needed a crutch. "Are you okay?" She held out her left hand for him to take.

Wendell couldn't speak. He swallowed. *Loser!*

"Can you walk me to my class?" she asked.

"How do I know *your* name? Everyone knows *your* name." Wendell locked his thumbs to his pockets. He looked at her extended hand as if could end world hunger, but inside his palm, behind his right fingers, rested the razored tip of the arrow.

"Please walk me to my class." Her voice went weak. Her eyes grew huge and filling. Midnight black. They pleaded. Her hand started to lower.

Why does your voice have to be weak? He wanted to ask. But he knew why.

He looked beyond her and out the door. They were alone now. He knew then that girls like this don't extend their hands to boys like him but once in a lifetime. So he reached out and let his right hand take hers. But he took her hand very carefully because the insert razor of the broad head went between their palms. He hadn't the time to hide the shaft up his arm. Nor had he the time to remove the cross razor that he had inserted to insure his stab into Mutt's neck would be fatal.

Wendell felt her fingers try to take his hand. He felt the hollow of her palm pulse around the weapon and a cold sweat develop on her fingers.

But then she held his hand tight.

He needed to say it. He wanted to tell her Mutt would soon be dead and that she was safe.

Instead of speaking, Wendell watched Deontra turn and stand in front of him. With eyes on his face, she released her hand from his and then she lifted and opened his palm. She looked down at the deadly arrowhead, secured tight by the tape. Her fingers felt the arrow shaft under his shirt. Then her finger traced over the razor. She then re-took his hand and interlocked her fingers with his, hiding the weapon and embracing how it dug and cut into her hand.

Their hands lowered and she gave a slight tug to get him moving in the direction of her class.

She held his hand tight during the walk. Her mind whirled. The razor in between them became the Blade of Demecluase.

Their hands moved in stride along their waists as Wendell escorted her to class, violating the school policy of keeping six inches between a girl and a boy.

Deontra stopped him only once in the empty hall. The tardy bell had sounded and all was still. She brought her right hand up along his chest and shoulder and rested her head against him and closed her eyes. She moved her left thumb along the razor and felt his free hand slid under her thick hair and gently pull her tighter.

She embraced her Death Angel.

He held her and felt her weakness because of his failure. Felt her shame because of his silence.

The moment ended and neither spoke. They walked on. Outside her door, she let go of his hand and watched him slid the arrow up along and back under his forearm and remove the smaller, inserted razor from the weapon.

Then she looked at him.

Wendell took a hard swallow, hoping he wouldn't gag on his tongue. "I failed you," he said. "I was there. I was supposed to rescue you."

She reached out a hand to his face and put her index finger against his lips. "Shhhh," Deontra said.

"I'm not done with killing…"

"Shhhh." She grew calm and a powerful peace rose up from her and came into him. Her other hand went to Wendell's and took the insert razor from him that he had just removed from the arrowhead. "Never focus on the forgiven," she said. Then she turned and entered her class.

Pamela opened her locker and screamed. Hearing this, she stopped and swung her embarrassed face left and right, searching for threats. She saw none.

Baffled students looked at her so she regained command, yanked the scare mask out of her locker and held it up for them to see.

"Ha! Ha! Ha!" Pamela goaded her neighbors. "Who's the wise guy?"

A few of her friends giggled at the joke, but none had guilt. They resumed between class tasks.

Pamela stepped nearly into her locker and put her hand on her heart. It was vibrating and she gulped breath. She knew why others ignored her startle. The furry thing was not a scare mask to them. But as she unfolded it, she saw that it was indeed the leather hide and fur face of a deer. She dropped it and smelled her hands. It was the mask that had come from a tangle of dark branches in fog vapor and hovered by her as bone-thick, curved claws scratched the glass on Ron's car window.

She shuddered and kicked the mask deep into her locker and purelled her hands. Only then did she see the typed note in the black lips of the deer face and knew the scare mask had another whisper. A chill came over her.

The last time the mask had spoken, it complimented her for rape-branding an innocent girl.

Pamela looked around.

Halls were emptying and she reached down took up the note. She unfolded it. As she read, the cold whisper from the mask seemed to come alive in the words.

Relaxxxx. Pamela's teacher won't see you tardy. Select an assembly tonight! Sacred Keg whispers stay strong! Remember where? Ron does! Here's the rules for tonight's celebration snare.

#1 Invite five leaders.
#2 Each leader invites two friends.
#3 Each friend invites one more.
Set the snare. Use the Keg as bait.
The killer will seek you.
He wants to kill you!
He will come!

As instructed, Pamela took a few personal minutes before going to Mr. Thompson's Gifted Government Class. She added some make-up to calm her eyes and dry the sweat on her face, then she walked to class. *Am I being hunted?*

Mr. Thompson met her directly outside his door. Behind him, his door was closed and the hall was empty.

"I'm sorry for being late," she said.

"It's a difficult time, isn't it?"

"Yes," she said, somehow feeling that it would be safer inside the class than with him in the hallway. Then she inhaled hard to hold her scream.

His gloved hand reached out to her, pointing one of it's

long, curled white claws at her. They were carved from what looked like the rib bones of deer. One claw went out and brushed hair from her forehead.

"That didn't take too long to re-powder I hope?" he whispered then scratched the claws down her shirt front.

She held still because the claws were so close to her.

"But…" she watched him take them off and drop them in his coat pocket.

"Careful," he said. "There's a monster around who wants to avenge Deontra. It's time to use a beast to fight a beast. It's time to use the Keg to catch the killer!" He smiled. "Sacred Keg needs you. Are you ready?"

"Yes," she said. She spoke with all her heart.

They crossed threshold and entered class.

Once in her chair, something dark tried to stir within her, but she took its energy and pitted it against things that upset her. Her bothersomes no longer seemed a threat. With her crime, authority and power had come her way! It was too good to be true.

Sherri saw the exchange between the teacher and Pamela. She was used to them. But this one *was* different and for some reason she wondered what Spam would say if *he* had seen it. Sherri saw Pamela stuff a paper into her pocket back at her locker. Was that what startled her friend? Or the teacher? *He didn't blindside Pamela, but he shook her up. Was it connected to the mask that made her jump at her locker?* Sherri looked at Pamela's pocket. She hated that pocket. It was where the Spam's obituary clippings were stored.

Mr. Thompson went to his desk and rummaged.

These students were waiting for his special blend of leverage and controversy.

But the man was pondering how much Mutt could take before he cracked. *Everybody can break. But his high card, the fugitive, Peter Mongrel, had been farming Weed Cave for decades!*

Gene relaxed. *Peter had good reason to insure that Mutt would ride this storm. But it must end soon.* He looked over his students again.

There was a secret lottery going on in the lounge at one hundred dollars per student entry. Teachers were gambling on pegging the killer. If the fund kept growing it would pass the betting on the NCAA Basketball Tournament!

And Gene didn't have confidence on any horse yet. He had placed no bet. This bothered him. It touched his pride. After decades, he had perfected the science of labeling teenagers. But the last day and a half had jilted him.

Gene faced class. *The killer is one of you. Why can't I see you? There is only three more hours of searching 'till the weekend. How long have you been stalking Mutt? Since Deontra? Since Deontra! Three premeditated murders since last Friday? Impressive! But the killer is going to have to go away! Too many strange cops. Too many questions. Too many of everything.*

Gene took a glance at his Gifted Class then thought about his upcoming 10th grade class that came after lunch. *That class has Spam in it. Spam had buried his brother, mother and father and he lives with a Vietnam Veteran who boasts about killing off the counties critters! Spam lives in death. Swims in it. Spam has been desensitized! I got my horse!*

Gene looked at his watch. His stomach growled in hunger. Real hunger. Stress always made Gene hungry. He thought of one his fat heifers. *A ribeye would be good about right now! But first I must protect my horse. Guilty or not, Spam's going down for murder and Carp with him! And I'll have my land back! Oh ya! Oh ya! Ya! Ya!*

"A Tremblen killed Fran, Tommy and Stanford." Gene told the class. That got their attention. Talk about a teaching hook. "But It's not a student so you can all relax," he smiled to set the stage.

"Who?" a kid asked.

"All I feel is that it's an adult. But I have no idea who. I want to listen to you play catch the bad guy. I want you to see how difficult it is. Let's profile someone. But not anyone real. How's this grab you for motive? It seems obvious that the Dog Pound did something really bad to someone who was very special and it was someone who really believes in justice and knows all about it!" Gene smiled.

Angie Stone raised her hand and he pointed to her. "Should we be talking about this? Captain Campbell said we should guard what we say."

"Well Miss Stone, good advice. Good advice, but this *is* Government Class. Sorry about that. Crime and Punishment is Chapter 16, so were going by our book. But since you raised your hand, Angie, and since this is the Gifted Class, do you mind if I mess around with you? Play the Devil's advocate?"

"Go ahead."

"Do you ever wonder what it would take to kill someone? Not with a paintball gun like in your church's little backyard game, but for real. What's that guy's name who comes around for lunch once in a while? Reveered? Do you see how easy and yet how hard it is? Yours *is* the church who does the paintball killing thing, right?"

"Yes," she answered. "It's our AGA."

"What's that?"

"After Game Activity," she seemed proud enough.

"What's your game called?"

"Holy War. And it's not a game really," she said. "It's about preparing Christians to die boldly for their faith. It's about martyr. Not murder."

"But you can't have one without the other! Can you?"

Thompson asked. "How do you prepare? You really use paintball guns to get yourself toughened up?"

"Yes, but. . ."

"Relax Angie," Mr. Thompson smiled. "I know you're not the killer. But can you see, from a law enforcement standpoint, from a crime and punishment eye, how you could become a suspect? Especially that Reveered character. I hear he's quite a good shot. I hear he's training a whole group on how to be handy with a gun. Does he ever use a bow and arrow?"

"I don't know. What are you saying?"

"I'm saying idealist are dangerous. They are more afraid of losing their little belief than death itself! If they are not afraid to die, well then *maybe* they are not afraid to kill. Understand?"

"I think so. Like our idealistic science teachers holding to their third dysfunctional marriage, *evolution*?" Angie asked.

"Smart girl! Now you're thinking. Good to know I have one class that still does that!" He smiled, but it was dangerous one, nevertheless. "Now Angie, if I may, that God in that big Bible of yours, has He, capital 'H', ever called people to be agents of his wrath? To kill? Take Moses for example. Wasn't he told to kill men, women and children and conquer some of those countries of the Middle East?"

"Actually the leader of that campaign was Joshua. Moses got fired, but…"

"So killing is okay if God says so? Maybe that's what our killer thinks. That's all I'm getting at. Right?"

"You're asking me if you're right?" Angie pressed. "Of course you're wrong! Moses and Joshua had the benefit of a Theocracy. God ran the government. God was with them in a cloud by day a pillar of fire by night. Otherwise their faces would have been melted off like in Indiana Jones! And the countries that the *Children* of Israel mowed over are said to have had negative birth rates. The excavation of Jericho had only adult bones mashed under those big walls. All those cities were Moloch cultures of death that had overflowed their Cup of Iniquity so to speak. Nearly like America with 59,622,917 babies sacrificed to the Gods of Convenience since Roe vs. Wade with the help of our 'Reproductive Health' Clinics or course." Angie used her fingers to put the clinic in quotation marks.

"Oh you Bleeding Heart Conservatives always sound like a broken DVD! Everything's always goes back to Roe vs. Wade! You lost. Hippies won! Get over it, Angie! All I'm asking is maybe the killer thinks he's God's agent of wrath. And what would that look like? Would he be religious? Hateful? Is he a Puker Rocker? Or does he just have pre-existing condition? Did his mom prop the milk bottle? Not breastfeed? He have a learning disorder? What comes after ODD or Opposition Defiance Disorder? MDPD? Murder Dog Pound Disorder? You guys should be able to figure this out. This here is the brightest mix of sophomore, juniors and seniors in the school. Now why not give back to Tremble. Why not hand over the killer? How hard can it be?"

Hands shot up across the room and some good theories were presented.

Mr. Thompson split class into groups and started making rounds. None challenged his secret Spam Theory or came up with one that could hold ice except his Holy War leader one. It was gaining some momentum and had Angie back on her heels.

As to Gene, he was thinking about getting his land back!

Pamela asked to be excused and Mr. Thompson made a rare exception. When it came to following governmental rules of school, he truly believed freedom came from obedience.

Then she asked him if Sherri could help her and he nodded again. No one noticed Mr. Thompson's sudden exception; the day was too strange to catch such details.

The two girl's went to Spam's locker. There, Pamela's dug into her pocket and snagged another obituary, some coins and cash, a crinkled typed note and a small role of tape.

"Let me hold your junk while you get the tape." Sherri cupped her hands.

"Thanks. What a day!" Pamela dumped her pocket stuffing into her friend's hands, retrieved the tape and used a long finger nail get it unrolling. Pamela stuck the last obituary of a man's death from liver failure to Spam's locker. She markered, DRUNK, across it.

Sherri saw Pamela's typed note and read the words on the backside of a fold:

… *won't see you tardy.*
…*Sacred Keg whispers.*
…*Ron does! See the…*

It wasn't much of a glance and Sherri turned her eyes down the hall, avoiding the common mistake of seeing forbidden knowledge and looking at the *examiner*. While she was looking away, Pamela saw her carelessness.

"Oh! I need that!" Pamela snatched the note and money.

"What?" Sherri asked, turning back.

"How do you like it?" Pamela pointed to the locker.

Sherri blinked at the news clipping sealed to the metal door with tape. She said nothing.

Pamela didn't expect her to.

Sherri was wondering if she was the only outsider, perhaps ever, to figure out Gene Thompson was the ghost controlling Sacred Keg.

Back in class, Sherri kept her eyes down. Scare and fear

made her do so. Where there was drugs and money there was power. Power hurt people. Students like her got crushed. She jumped when someone knocked on the door.

A deputy framed the doorway as a student opened it.

Teacher Thompson was across the room. "Who is next on your Q & A, deputy?"

"That would be you, Mr. Thompson, would you care to come with me for a few moments?"

An office secretary was behind the deputy.

Gene Thompson was about to be questioned. "I beg your pardon?" Mr. Thompson asked.

"You need to come with me."

"This is a Government Class! You come inside and we'll make it a teaching experience!"

The deputy entered. "I'm a deputy from across the state. A few of us were called in to lend a hand."

"How special. Do you have a name, deputy?"

"You are Mr. Thompson and reside at 515 Forest Drive?"

"Yes." Gene came in front of the class and motioned two students out of their seats. He and the deputy sat. "And you are?"

"Deputy Weary, Mr. Thompson."

A shiver went up Gene and he folded down the hairs on his arm. *Weary! That man is a deputy now! He must be a hundred pounds lighter than the cop we ran out of town four years ago.* Thompson looked up at the clock. He must survive the next five minutes. "I'm trying to place your name," Gene said.

"And you have lived at that address since 1962?"

"Hang in there. I'm trying to place your name."

"No you're not. Cut the crap. I didn't buy it when I sat in that chair over there," the deputy pointed. "And I don't buy it now! I'm the deputy who wanted you arrested for the rape and murder of my sister. I wanted you charged with Criminal Sexual Conduct on minors. I wanted you arrested for harvesting and distributing illegal narcotics. For poisoning the children of Tremble. Ring a bell you filthy liar?"

"Now I remember. Wow! You've lost a ton of weight. But as to those charges? They were so far fetched that *your* chief fired you. And the Mayor ran you out of Tremble with your tail between your legs before I even got wind of it all. Do you remember that? Do you want me to help you remember more? Maybe the class wants to hear some of your family history. As short as it is."

"Maybe the class wants to here how Tremble High School has 75% less drug related problems as all other schools in Michigan."

"Maybe other schools should learn from us!" Mr. Thompson said.

Students clapped and rapped their desk. "Go Thompson!" One yelled.

"Are you serious?" Deputy Weary asked. "You mean other Michigan schools should establish a dirty Government teacher to poison children with pharmaceutical grade illegal narcotics? And control the police and town? Make his own dirty harem? Other towns should do that?"

"I beg you pardon?" Thompson asked.

"You'll be begging for more than that when I'm through with you, Thompson!" Deputy Weary said. "You'll be begging." Weary turned to the class.

One girl looked out the window as if this bored her. She was acting.

Another was frightened and dropped her eyes to her desk.

Both wore cheerleading uniforms.

Deputy Weary was on his feet and going to the door.

"You're done with the interrogation?" Thompson asked. "And the threats? Don't end it like that! Where's the massaging and friendly bantering to go along with your disrespectful, hateful slander?"

Weary reached for the door, opened it, stepped to it then stopped and drilled his stare at the two cheerleaders. Some things never change.

One, the smart one, kept her eyes on the teacher.

But the other? She didn't know where to look because she didn't expect the cop stare.

All Sherri did know is how the cop saw right into her heart.

Deputy Weary saw truth. He saw what he came looking for. And when he saw it, he ended the interrogation and closed the door behind him.

"Ladies and Gentleman, students of government, welcome to Chapter 16, Crime and Punishment and Law Enforcement 101. If you were bullied in school, you become a bully cop," Mr. Thompson said.

Hands rose.

Thompson pointed to Pamela.

"Who's Detective Weary?" she asked as if someone had just pulled her string.

"Deputy Weary," Thompson corrected. "He's no Detective, young lady. He's the survivor of his sister's suicide. Deputy Weary is Spam's Uncle who had to leave the Tremble area or face criminal charges for stalking, harassment, criminal trespass, negligence and abuse."

"Did you file the charges?" a boy asked.

"No. But maybe I should have. As a matter of fact, I think this is the first time we actually talked with each other."

Sherri kept her eyes down and disinterested. She was scared more than ever and felt the teacher trying to hedge her to engage, trying to flank her to see what was on her mind. She felt Thompson knew her secret too.

Behind Sherri, a blond haired boy dared to scratch his eye for the first time. He knew any contact could start them gushing in tears of stress. And movement would attract Thompson like a bug on a pond's surface would a bass. Wendell saw that cop rip into his teacher and rattle the man to the bone. Any hope that he could survive any questions from a cop were now gone. He now held his hands under the desk and out of sight.

Thompson was still up there! Questions could still come! It *was* the gifted class after all.

The girl in front of him was a cheerleader. A very pretty one. She put her hand and rubbed the back of the her friend who seemed upset. "Relax Sherri," Pamela rubbed harder on the girl's back.

Wendell watched the slender fingers caress the girl's back. They were both pretty. But the captain, Pamela. Beautiful.

"Relax," Pamela said again, softer than before.

Sherri looked back at her.

Wendell held still, but it made no difference. He was invisible to girls like these.

The class was on a different topic.

"You okay?" Pamela asked Sherri.

Sherri looked at her, revealing nothing.

"It's okay. Bam Bam can handle all of this mess and more!" Pamela winked at Sherri.

Behind them, Wendell held still. Very still. He was in the presence of the monster who drove the Dog Pound to rape Deontra.

His arrow under his arm came alive. It seemed to coil back like a scared viper that wanted nothing else but to sink it's fangs into the neck of Pamela and spray her blood across the eight desks around her.

But Wendell never unleashed the weapon. Sweat broke

across his face but he knew better than to move in Thompson's class because the teacher zeroed in on movement. *It had to be wrong! All wrong! Girl's like her can't be killed. She's no dog. No carnivore! No rapist!*

But then it happened inside of Shyly. He felt it grow. His hand clenched into a fist. Again, for as many times in as many weeks, he knew it was all wrong. That it was all bad. He watched Deontra being attacked.

Over and over.

And he knew that he had to make it right.

He *would* kill Mutt.

And he would find something special for Bam Bam. Something *worse* than death.

20
God, Government & OOB

Pamela saw Spam's group her first step into the cafeteria and she felt led to go to Angie Stone. The two girls were polite to each other over the years, but had never really talked. Now with murders upon Tremble High, enhanced by Spam and especially his uncle in last class, consternation was pushing alpha leaders to dialogue.

"What do you think of Spam?" Pamela asked Angie, nodding to where Spam sat with twenty-five students around him.

"I don't know what to think about *him*. You?"

"Nothing, really," Pamela said, "But he's God-talking to them. What's he saying anyways?" Pamela smiled and then got called away. She left Angie. *Poor Angie, leader of Tuesday's Before School Bible Group and defender of life in Thompson's class, was now being disrespected by Spam who was shepherding sheep without her permission!*

Angie Stone sat up and became concerned. *Spam's only a sophomore! He's in the upperclassmen lunch! Again! How could he be a leader and violate school rules?* She then felt convicted to confront Spam. She made it her mission to know who was and who wasn't a Christian at Tremble High. And she never heard anything of this Spam until yesterday. She made a mental note to check his wrist.

Quarterback Ron Robertson saw six players in his starting lineup for tonight's big game listening to Spam. *I don't believe it! Coach is gonna...* Ron pushed strong fingers through thick blond hair. *Maybe I'm not leadership material.* His lip furled and teeth bit down. Now it was personal. His 6'6" frame stood. He patted his friends hard on the back to make sure they observed the lesson. He nodded for one boy to follow just in case.

Several of Ron's solid teammates were now sitting with Spam as well as some scrubs. *Why are they listening to Spam after I told them not to?* Ron approached.

"You boy's already blew one practice! What do you hope to accomplish? If you boy's don't respect me off the field, you won't honor the program in tonight's big game!" Ron stopped at the edge of the gathering and gave the players around Spam the Leadership Nod. "We need to get things straight!"

Spam kept speaking as he answered a question. He ignored Ron, which the captain construed as *disrespectful*.

Everyone else around Spam was just amazed at his logic about God stuff. Students were rooted to their seats.

Nearby tables saw tension. They nudged others. It had the makings of a main event.

Ron circled, looking for a chair.

Spam was referencing three news clippings, circulating through the group.

All were grade-schoolers when Spam's brother was burned alive.

"The fire is what changed my goals in life from those about comfort to ones of discipline," Spam answered.

"Why would you want that?"

"When I act with discipline, I know it pleases God."

"What's so good about that?"

"It helps me hate selfishness. God hates selfishness. It's disobedience. He calls it sin. Through my discipline I respect God. When I obey, I am free."

"But God allowed your brother to burn!" someone said.

Not finding a seat, Ron lifted a weaker teammate by jersey scuff right off a chair and sat next to Spam. Front and center.

"Yes," Spam said through Ron as if the QB was a vapor. "I *was* very mad at God. Not any more. Now I'm hurt and sad. But sadness proved fertile ground for my soul to find God. Without that, I don't know if I could have been changed."

"Is that why you wanted the school to be sad for the murdered?" another asked.

"Yes. We must always fight against our orientation to self-protect and indulge. God wants us to stay vulnerable and weak."

"And you're telling me that's better?" a boy asked who looked weak, trampled and vulnerable.

"Anything that helps us hear God's whisper is good. Weakness before God is power. It creates a spine of steel. And spines of steel are the only one's that walk the streets of gold."

"And you have a spine of steel, Spam?" the Football Captain asked, declaring his ignored presence to Spam. His eyes were inches from Spam's. Now in the spotlight, he threw his heavy arm around Spam in a mock embrace. "If you're that strong, we could use you on the football team!" He stared around. "But we better not have any open spots!"

Spam met Ron's eyes.

"You're looking at me funny, Spam!" Ron said.

Someone laughed.

"I'm not a girl you know! I can prove it!"

Still Spam stared.

"And if you're teaching my players the ins and outs of how the turn their other cheek and take it in the rear, well, I have a problem with that too!" Ron flashed smile and more laughed on impulse. Ron's smile was so friendly and personable. He was a natural leader.

Cops enjoyed Ron. A few watched. *That QB has style. He'll get those hooky brats back where they belong.*

More heads turned.

Half the cafeteria was now watching.

Curiosity was rising.

Ron knew it, he needed it and he kept his arm around Spam as he waited for everyone to catch up. Get on the same page. Hear the same signal. Soon he would lead them to boo his teammates out of the Spam Zone. His hand now clamped around the base of Spam's neck to insure puppetry response.

"How about it Spam? You teaching these boys how to get themselves spanked?" Ron's voice boomed over the entire area. He used the tone that thousands of fans heard when he barked commands on the football field. He nodded Spam's head to agree.

Little Angie Stone was in Spam's circle. She had come and had been waiting for Spam to make a theological mistake so she could rebuke him and lead his sheep back to green pastures and still waters. She saw Ron's vice grip crunching Spam's neck. Saw Ron's muscles push out veins under his skin like pencils. *Ron's closing the heretic's mouth! God sure works in wonderful ways!*

But Spam, inches away from Ron's ear, eeked a whisper. "You're a coward," Spam said and flushed red as Ron's tightening, sealed further comments. He was losing blood because Ron shut it done so he could do his magic.

"What did you call me?" Ron whispered back and had to let up his grip, so Spam could catch air and respond.

Spam faced Ron.

Few could hear but Angie Stone was sitting very close.

"You're a coward," Spam said. Words raspied and air-restricted came out. "A chicken who plays the victim card, you can justify…"

Ron clamped Spam's neck shut, cutting air supply and vocals. His fingerpads swelled with bloodlust and he scanned the cafeteria for escape. He wanted to toss Spam like a football. He saw his Pamela, two tables over, looking nervous and shaking her head in caution. Ron came back to Spam.

"You think you can't get hurt because there are fifty cops at school?" Ron said, genuinely not knowing what to do. "If this ever gets out, I'll…"

"Spam called Ron a coward!" Small Angie Stone's voice was shrill and loud and very clear. No one could have ever expected such boom from such a tiny girl. But she felt the truth must be told. And if Spam was big enough to whisper it, it was her job to broadcast it. She roared out the words as if her lungs made up half her body weight.

Ron's heart sunk four inches. He dropped Spam like a rag doll and nodded to his tag-a-long who could have been a top athlete if he wasn't a discipline case. The snake-eye kid put an ear to Ron.

Ron had to make a real-time, split-second decision. "Kill him! One month free," Ron said into the fighter's ear.

The cruel one lunged and was immediately over Spam, who was sitting. He gouged his left hand under Spam's chin to frame the blow.

Ron walked away.

Everyone in the cafeteria suddenly stood up. Many stepped onto tables. Authority recognized energy downburst, but found themselves outside the crowd. Too late. They started to claw to the core of conflict.

Ron was leaving and bumped into the lead staff, causing a pile-up. "Excuse me," he said. He stepped in front again. He said it again, his wide body blocking the aisle.

The attacker struck hard with meat hook swing, splitting Spam's top and bottom lips, knocking him backwards, flat on the table. Then the invader jumped on Spam. Knowing time was short, he waited to get the perfect shot. His right arm was cocked way back, and his knees were in Spam's chest. His left hand grasped Spam's bloodied chin. He knew Spam was shaken, but alert, yet he saw Spam take no defense.

Spam saw his aggressor and held still, head against the table. He became indifferent to his outcome.

The attacker struck. He punched hard and there was nowhere for the impact energy to be deflected. Knuckles went deep into Spam's face, sinking in just below the nose and cutting out three front teeth and setting them afloat in a mouth of blood. He took aim to strike again, but then Spam's eyes gave an expression the cruel one had never seen. The fist lowered because there was no fear in the one being beaten. For a moment, he wanted to apologize, but then cops tackled him.

Officer Oink whipped out cuffs and rattled them above his head before he clamped them on. He yanked the boy to his feet.

"But he started it!" The boy said but passion was gone from his voice. He tried to say it again to keep focus off his quarterback, but he didn't have to.

Everyone was looking at Spam.

On the tabletop, Spam rolled onto a shoulder, turned his head to one side and lowered his chin. He opened his mouth and let his teeth spill out with giant globs of red, Jell-O-like blood. It all splattered on a white plate. Blood drooling from the corners of Spam's mouth, he winked at Angie and smiled. He sat up half way until bloodrush spun the ceiling.

Two teachers reached in to stabilize, but fingers retracted at the sight blood. "Someone go get some gloves please!" one yelled. Since they couldn't help Spam because of risk of blood born pathogens in accordance to OSHA Health Standards, they did the next best thing. They stopped others from aiding.

Spam lost equilibrium and fell back, head cracking on the

table so hard it tipped over a carton of milk.

Pamela saw peers and it was not good. Yesterday Spam had influence, now he had something else. And whatever it was, it was something that scared Pamela.

Then and there she decided Spam had gone far enough. Mr. Thompson had given her the power to bring leaders together and she would to deal with Spam her way. Get rid of him once and for all. Send him back into his despair. No Spam or any other canned meat was going to dethrone her ability to reap the rewards of running tap on Sacred Keg. She would only invite leaders to tonight's sacred gathering who had as much to lose as herself. And deep down, she knew that Thompson was planning something too.

A teacher shoved the lounge door open and pressure-hissed it all the way to the doorstop.

Heads turned.

"You're not going to believe what just happened out there!" She was met with semi-inquisitive expressions. But no one spoke. It was a long-standing rule that no one talked of students in the lounge. There was hesitation. It was a union thing.

"Spit it out." Gene Thompson said.

"Spam is still spitting it out."

"Like yesterday? Missing class again?" a lady was offended.

"No. Well, maybe. Today he just. . ." she met the coach's eye. "Spam just called Ron Robertson a coward."

Coach's hand had just released a quarter into the vending and pushed the button.

All was still.

A twenty ounce bottle of Coke™ clanged into the machines dispenser.

All watched as coach slowly took hold of his Coke and nearly tore it in half as it came from the vending machine. He stood up slow and stepped forward. "What happened?"

"Nothing good," the teacher said.

Gene Thompson turned back to his lunch. He was pleased. Bad news for Spam meant good news for him. He always said he wasn't in drugs for the money, but he was down a ton of money with all these cops around Mutt.

With Mutt out of commission until the cops got the killer, it was getting worse every minute. But everything about the cheerleader felt promising.

It always had.

And the good news? No one would ever think about betting on a horse named Spam!

Coach twisted off the cap and took a few chugs and left the room. Everyone was still. The door closed.

Gene looked at his food. *This Spam kid is doing it with Carp's help! That widow-land-swindler's grooming a leader?* Gene rubbed his chin. *"Me and Carp share a border. How much does Carp know? And it's a lot harder to make a leader than to make a killer.*

Mr. Thompson watched OOB parade the cuffed punk towards the patrol car. He had come alongside in a manner that seemed accidental. Above him was a blue Michigan sky and the grass of the school lawn sparkled green because it was a warm day. Red leaves rustled in the few maple trees that were planted in memory of two students killed in a car crash in 1984. Beyond them, three flagpoles bannered their emblems.

"Officer Brighton, may I have a word with you if you please?"

OOB opened the back door of his cruiser and guided the boy into the cage, holding the assailant's head so the boy's noggin didn't thump the metal car roof. "I have to book him for assault," OOB said. "It's a pretty busy day."

"Understood," Thompson said. "But I think I have a lead and I want the credit to go to the city and not the county."

Officer Oink Brighton slammed the door and stepped forward, pulling out a pad for notes. He clicked his pen, ignoring the small fish because a White Whale just spouted off his bow! He knew Thompson could smell a rat better than a piper. "Fire away."

"Remember that serial killer kid out east a few years back?"

"Which one?"

"The one raised in a slaughter house? A pig slaughter house?"

"Yes."

"The shrinks say that seeing all that blood and pig screaming bent that kid's mind into a killer."

"If you say so."

"I do. I want you to take a close look at Spam."

"That's who this kid just pounded."

"You don't say. Well, that fits."

"Fits what?"

"Who would think to investigate a victim for murder?"

"Spam?"

"What do you know of Dr. Carp?"

"The Vet? Come on," Brighton took out his keys, as if he had to worry about the boy overheating in the back seat.

"What *do* you know about John Carp?"

"Well, as a matter of fact I was by his place about a week ago. Last Sunday."

"Did you know Carp was discharged from the U.S. Military in Vietnam for murdering his patients?" Thompson extended a file to OOB that said, 'CONFIDENTIAL' on it. "It's public record. He's a *murderer*. He *kills* off the counties old pets. He collects *roadkill* for all of DOT. And who helps him *kill* all those unwanted pets and dispose of the dead?"

"Spam!" Brighton saw the sparkle.

"Spam right!" Thompson said. "Run it by Chief. I might be wrong and hopefully I am. That boy's been through it."

"*Burned* up his brother. Seen his mom and pop die *wrong*," Brighton said. "I should've *seen* that."

"It's not your job to solve it. And how could you see it, when your beat is dealing with punks like this?"

OOB nodded and pointed at Mr. Thompson.

Thompson nodded a back-at-ya to Brighton.

OOB lifted the file. "How'd you get this?"

"You dug it up at the V.A. Memorial Hospital. It bothers you when you see an adult like Carp take kids under their wing who aren't kin, doesn't it?"

OOB nodded.

"It would make it better for me as a teacher not be involved in the cracking of the case."

OOB nodded again, bunching up his nose and forcing his eyes apart. He took up his car key and gestured locking his lips.

Thompson nodded.

OOB nodded back, crossed around the front of his car, entered it and spun gravel as he chirped the tires on the pavement.

21

Milk Maids & Library Aids

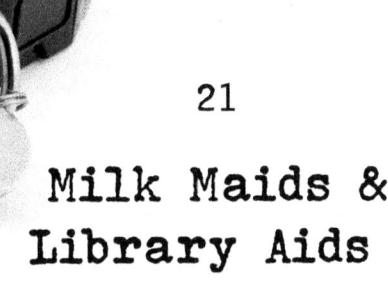

Thief Ryan Knack stole stuff with Watson. He did it because he needed to go to the Land Down Under to get away from people who drove him over the top. The very appeal of leaving Michiganders was all it took. Escapism had become his religion. It was an intolerance issue, but right now his mind was like a stretched out rubberband. He had lost his elasticity. Ryan wanted to be patient, relaxed, carefree and uninvolved.

He had listened to Watson explain how not to take stuff personal. He was indifferent about the murders of the Mutts and the football boycott and pretty much whatever else was happening in and around Tremble.

But something happened to Ryan Knack when that player beat Spam. It brought up some issues.

Ryan had never talked to her in his life. She was a cute little cheerleader and he was a PB&J eating thief. He could live with that. He knew who he was, but now he wanted to know who *she* was.

It'd be rough being with a girl from the founcy, but the way she carried Spam's bloody plate back to the kitchen, compelled him to follow her. To know her.

"My name's Ryan," he said from behind a normal head of sandy brown hair.

"Mine's Sherri." She put the tray down, looking at the blood.

"Why did you bring the tray up?" he asked.

"I'm not doing anything wrong!" Sherri said. "I'm sorry to

say that. It's just that things are strange."

"It was wrong, wasn't it?" he asked.

Her eyes looked up at his and she was afraid.

Afraid of what, Ryan didn't know, but it bothered him. A girl as pretty as Sherri shouldn't have to be afraid of nothing. "Your friends hate Spam? Why is that?"

"I don't know. But I like him," she said. "Your name's Ryan, right?"

He nodded.

"Well, if they found out I'd… How'd it get so weird?" She was relieved and her aurora seemed to warm the area.

He lifted the plate from the tray and swirled the blood as if panning for a gold tooth. "Dunno. Where's the teeth?" The cafeteria was empty, except for a girl with long black hair, lingering near Spam's Ground Zero. She was holding a milk carton.

A door slammed.

Sherri jumped.

Ryan didn't like that. *A girl as pretty as you shouldn't have to jump for nothing.* "I'm going for Frank after school in Fight Zone," he said, referring to spot where students could really tear into each other without interruption. "Maybe I'll see you around?"

"Okay," she ran her index finger on the edge of Spam's tray.

"I'm going to beat down their strongest for what they did to the weakest." Ryan Knack returned a smile. *What's the difference? I'll be in Australia in a few weeks!*

"Come with me to Sacred Keg after the game?" Sherri asked.

"You sure? The Keg! I mean, don't you want to save your invitation for another? After I'm done with Frank, I won't be welcome."

"Maybe we'll do something else then."

"Sound's like we just invited each other," he said.

They parted.

Sherri didn't feel too good. She liked this Ryan. She sensed his calming effect and she felt safe standing next to him. Very safe. Too bad he was fighting Big Frank. It would be a long and painful rehab for Ryan. She wondered when visitation hours ended at the hospital.

Deontra gave Spam his teeth back. She had followed teachers to Ground Zero, found the teeth and put them into a carton of milk and then went on the hunt. She found Spam in the nurse's station, sitting on a cot, waiting for some ice.

"This is for you," Deontra said, extending the milk to him.

He waved it off. "Nof firsty."

"It's not to drink, Spam, it's your teeth." She laughed. "Milk potassium keeps the roots alive. Do you know a dentist?"

Another boy showed up. "You okay, Spam?"

Spam nodded.

"Sorry about what happened."

"Why?"

"Because you got hurt."

"I also thook a stand. Ya can't do one without the other."

"Nice connection, Spam! My name is Luke, do you know me?" He looked at Spam then Deontra and dropped his eyes. "I mean, does Spam know me. Of course, you know, you're not going to know me."

Deontra smiled, knowing that she had never seen him before.

"Do you haf a car?" Spam asked the boy.

"No."

"I do," Deontra said.

Spam took the milk, got down and steadied himself and

felt Luke hold him upright. They both followed Deontra out of the office, out of the school and into the parking lot. "Where'd you fark your far at?" Spam asked.

"Wait!" Luke looked at Spam. "Come the Holy War tonight!"

"What's that?"

"A paintball, capture the flag, end of the world type game. We play it at Reveered's. He lives on that creek off Forest Ave above town. Below Thompson land."

Spam looked at him and winced. The pain was killing him and he wiped blood that leaked out the side of his mouth. Spam shrugged his shoulders. "What thime?"

"After the football game." He looked back at school when the bell rang.

"Nice meeting you Luke," Deontra said.

Luke left.

"Leth go," Spam said.

At this Deontra laughed again in an innocent way. "You talk funny with no teeth, Spam." Seeing twice that he had trouble standing straight, she took hold of his arm and opened the car door for him.

Once on the road, he pointed where to go. Pain was sharp. He felt every bump. In the Vet's driveway he looked at her. "You might want to go back."

"To where? School?" She became intrigued. "What are we doing here?" She opened her door, stepped out and joined him.

He pointed up the steps.

She slowed, as rumors came upon her and looked at Spam. "Is this Carp's Kill Clinic?"

"Hef's a little low on social skills. Fhaf's why we get along," Spam said and entered.

She followed him in.

Doc was on the phone. He gave Spam a look and started laughing.

Spam blushed.

Deontra smiled and looked at her feet.

"You can sit down if you want," Doc said to the girl.

"I'm not going to sit down." Deontra's nose was turned up and Spam looked around for a dog turd on a chair or something.

Spam deducted it could be anything.

Doc hung up.

"Smart girl to not sit around here. It was a trick question. What happened?" Doc asked. "You people finally learning how to hooky rooky?"

Spam smiled but the man missed it because he was looking at the girl.

"Smile for him again, Spam," Deontra said.

The boy did so.

Carp saw. Then he took the boy's head in his hands, like he would a horse, and pulled the lips back.

"You got the teeth in there?" Doc nodded to the milk, still looking into the mouth.

Spam tried to nod his head through the grasp of the old man. "Ahhh Hahh," he said.

The man let go and walked to the operating table and wiped off some hair with a rag.

Spam trudged up, then climbed without being prompted.

Deontra followed.

Doc flipped on surgery lights and pushed Spam to lay back. "Suppose things haven't changed much. How long ago?" Doc yanked down the operating light, pulled Spam's head back and beamed it on the bloody craters in the mouth.

"Twenty minutes." Deontra helped, seeing Doc's fingers prodding into Spam's gums.

"Good!" He pushed Spam's mouth open again.

Semi-embarrassed, Spam looked at her from down on the stainless table.

The girl tried to smile but stopped.

Spam lurched in pain.

"You better take some Happy Air," Doc said. He took up some disinfectant wipes and started fingering pet slime out of a cone-shaped cylinder that he had custom made from an Evian™ bottle for big dogs. Then he used several alcohol swabs on the bottle. It had a tube duct taped into the drinking end. He looked at the girl. "You wanna turn that valve?" he asked.

She did.

Doc got Spam inhaling.

Deontra became disturbed.

Carp looked at her. "Did a girl do this?" Carp asked, nodding to Spam's missing teeth.

Deontra could tell the old man was nervous from her being there.

"No. A football player did."

Relieved, Doc smiled and seemed to want to celebrate.

"You guys get combat pay for studying at Tremble High?"

"Tell me about it," Deontra said and looked away.

Doc sensed she was no stranger to pain as he held gas to Spam's face, watching the boy on the table relax. Then he turned back to Deontra.

"Want some gas?"

"Would it help my ribs?"

"What happened?" he asked as he gassed Spam out.

She told him.

"Gimme a minute for the teeth. Then we'll do an X-ray on you."

"Here?" she looked around.

"Hey! Careful what you hack on. Don't criticize the future of American Health Care."

With Spam absent from his last class, the fire went out of Mr. Thompson's search for the slayer. The teacher never bothered to widen the net and he was tired. He stared at the wimpy sophomores discussing justice and fizzled out from lack of energy. Near the end of class, he realized most of the talk was still about Spam.

The fight between Ryan Knack and Big Frank at Fight Zone, promised carnage and students flocked, hoping adults wouldn't catch wind. Ryan knew the punk who thrashed little Spam had been sent to the tank. So he headhunted the biggest jock on the team.

Big Frank.

After Ryan and Frank finished round three of monologue, over fifty students crowded them.

"You're siding with Spam?" Frank concluded. "Against me?"

"And you're siding with the coward. And that's always painful," Ryan said.

Frank rushed.

Ryan stepped into it. And although Ryan wasn't an athlete, he was plenty athletic. Ryan had bulk in his V-shaped body, topping scales at one-eighty. But how he moved surprised everyone.

No one saw him step into the big lineman's arching punch. No one saw him move.

Ryan's right wrist parried down Frank's big, right hand, meat-hook, clobber-style swing. And his left palm knocked

Frank's right elbow upward. The arm twist sent Frank sprawling into the brick wall.

Frank's head struck hard and he fell to the cement. His feet woke up first and scurried to find footing like a dog on ice. His skull donged like a bell.

Frank stayed down only for a moment then sat up. He shook his head and looked at the red splatch of blood on concrete. His hand reached to his head and came back bloody.

With a little more torque, Ryan could have leveraged Frank's entire weight against that brick wall and could have given him a descent concussion. But Ryan didn't want to injure Frank. He wanted to hurt him.

The football lineman shook his neck again as if he had to snap it back in place and stood up.

"You can walk away now, Frank," Ryan said. "I've no beef with you, but it's not fair for me to take it out on any other of your teammates because they are all too weak and pathetic. Ron included."

"Keep talking," Frank walked up to Ryan.

They circled.

Ryan backed up to the brick wall.

"Where you going?" Frank asked.

Ryan's back bumped up against the wall. Beyond Frank he saw over fifty students. He tried to see Sherri, but couldn't. That was good.

Sherri was a nice girl.

Ryan came off the wall, hands down and palms out, signaling a draw.

Frank shoved him hard against the wall.

Ryan bounced off of it, staying upright and balanced.

"It'll be Shock and Awe," Frank said.

"Don't miss," Ryan said. "This wall will break your knuckles." He pushed out at Frank's chest in a slow, playful manner.

Frank nodded and took his advice and grabbed a handful of Ryan's shirt with his left hand. Frank looked in Ryan's eyes.

Ryan was calm.

Frank had to admit that Ryan was calm. Almost too calm. He felt his fingers clench tight the shirt. He felt them stretch the fabric.

Ryan held still, palms out wide and open. He knew Frank's big right round house swing would finish him. But he also knew Frank was leery of the wall.

Frank knew it too. Behind his back, the football player again curled his right hand into a fist as his left pressed Ryan to the wall. "No room now for your funk," Frank said.

Ryan lifted his left hand out, open palmed as if to ward off Frank's blow.

Frank smirked. "Good night, Ryan!"

Ryan's left hand clenched Frank's hand that had the handful of shirt and clamped it harder to his shirt and chest. He did this while his right hand grabbed Frank's left elbow and pulled Frank's arm harder into his chest.

"What's this?" Frank asked, his right arm still drawn back for the slug-of-the-century.

Ryan smiled. He bent his waist towards Frank then released his knees and dropped all his weight.

Frank's left wrist, tangled and pinned to Ryan's body was no match for the angle or the 180 lb. drop.

It snapped.

Frank screamed and air burst forth from his lungs, spewing spit and phlegm in agony. It was a very high scream. A shrill.

Ryan, back standing and in control of the broken wrist, twisted it and dead dropped Frank on his back again and their was no mercy this time. The head never bounced off the concrete.

Frank was down.

Down hard.

Girls screamed, making one of those echoes that last about a decade or so.

It wasn't Ryan's idea of a good time to injure someone. Let along injure them bad. But when he had to do it, he did what he felt must be done. And he finished the job. He conquered, leaving no room for upheaval. "Can you say, Ron's a coward?" Ryan stepped over Frank and asked, looking down at him.

Blood was gone from Frank's expression. It had better places to rush to. Sweat and foam leaked from the skin stretched over Frank's face and pooled in the eye sockets and soaked his hair.

Ryan looked around. All was still. He pointed to a football player wearing a jersey. "Get his feet elevated if you want to help him. He might go into shock." Ryan found Sherri and they left together.

Watson and Ron just stared at each other.

Pamela was stunned as her teammate left with Ryan. She turned to Watson as others started to drift away. The two moved away from Frank.

Ron came up to them. Pamela gave Ron and Watson some details on Keg, but none felt like celebrating.

Sacred Keg couldn't come soon enough.

They were losing control.

Mutt had come back to school in his mom's car but never left the parking lot. Never left the locked car. He watched Ryan and Sherri leave Fight Zone and smiled. Seeing Ryan leave unscathed and with a pretty girl only meant one thing. *Big Frank tried to fight fair.* He exhaled some smoke. *If you want*

to beat Ryan in a fight you better put a bullet into him first!

But Mutt didn't care much about any little battle. He was in a war! Looking in the shadows, opposite the distraction, his eyes searched for the killer who was trying to ambush him. *Someone, who wants to kill me, is very close. If a murderer can poison and shoot my friends, then he can kill me anyway he wants to! Maybe Deontra has found an avenger!*

The thought shocked him.

Then it made sense.

Little Deontra knows my killer?

All was quiet in the hallways because school had been over for ten minutes. Athletes were in the locker rooms. Commuters and bus riders had boarded and drove away. A lone janitor pushed along a wide broom, scraping lose paper and trash over the floor. The ambulance had just taken Frank away. Some teachers were in the office area, discussing how a star football player could have broken his wrist and got a concussion by slipping at a drinking fountain.

And Angie Stone walked onward and upward toward the library, carrying her heavy burden as if it were a cross. She creaked the door open and three sheriff deputies and a police officer looked her way.

With no significant leads to speak of, a deputy came to her. He motioned over a female staff and together the three of them sat. "What's on your mind?" he asked after they sat.

Angie looked at her feet.

The deputy waited. He and his staff interviewed over eighty students and got nothing. Absolutely nothing! To his knowledge, she was the first student to come forward. He liked her timing too. He knew she came late because she didn't want to be seen. "No matter how insignificant it seems, all information on these murder cases is important," he said.

"Really?"

He nodded. "What's your name?"

"Angie. Angie Stone."

"Your address."

"319 Central."

"Do your parents know you're here?"

"Yes. My mom does."

"Why isn't she here?"

"I don't know. She has stuff to do."

"Does she know the information you want to tell us?"

"Yes."

"Did she tell you to come forward?"

"Yes."

"Is she the only adult to encourage you?"

At this Angie hesitated, allowing enough time for the note-taker to glance at the deputy. "Yes," Angie said.

Lie! The deputy thought.

"What is it? Broad stroke it at first then focus on details if possible."

"Our group, RBY, meets every Friday for AGA. We meet at our leader's house. His name is Reveered."

"What's RBY?"

"Oh. Regular Baptist Youth."

"And AGA?"

"After Game Activity."

"Reveered?"

"He's the leader. He and his wife, but mainly him."

Deputy nodded. "His real name?"

"Henry Witherbean. Maybe Wutherbean. We just call him Reveered."

"Why?"

"That's what I'm trying to say. He's deadly. He hurts someone almost every week with his paintball gun."

"Is he on staff with your church?"

Angie huffed. "Oh no. No way. He's a volunteer leader."

"Is he a youth pastor?"

"Sometimes he's called that, but not by me. He doesn't have enough theological training."

"Why are you telling us this?"

"That's why I'm here! That's what I'm getting at. Now, I may be wrong. But I think he's the killer. It's his role at AGA to kill those who violate his belief. At AGA he's the one who kills the Christians. For pretend, I mean."

"We're the murdered boys Christians at AGA?"

"Them. The Dog Pound? Of course not! Ours is a church activity!"

"Yet, you're saying Reveered's a murderer?"

"Well, I mean, at AGA he is. And a good one. He says he thinks he's strong enough to die for God and, well, you know, maybe he's strong enough to kill for God too."

"Why would God want him to kill those boys?"

"I don't know."

"You sure?"

She nodded. "You find that out and it will help you get the killer."

The deputy dropped his notepad on the desk and looked around the empty library at the remainder of his team packing files for the afternoon meeting. He turned to Angie. "Are you saying your youth pastor is a murderer?"

"I can't come right out and say it, because I don't know for sure. He's always in camo and hiding wherever in ambush. You know?" she nodded.

"And you have AGA tonight?"

"I wanted to cancel and have an EPBM but *Reveered* wanted AGA instead." She looked at the deputy as if it was hard for even *her* to believe.

"What's EPBM?"

"Emergency Prayer and Bible Meeting?"

"How much have you been with Reveered?"

"This week?"

He nodded.

"Well, we were at his house last Friday for AGA, but of course it ended early because he shot Luke in the neck." She lowered her chin. "It could have been serious. Then we met at his house on Thursday for EPBM but, of course, all he wanted to do was hear about the murders and, oh, of course he wanted to hear all about Spam. Spam's the one who basically killed off his family seven years back." She said this in case he was one of those deputies who had come to help from far away.

"Who was all there? At EBPM and AGA?"

"At AGA it just the teenagers from our church. But EPBM had some others. They were invited."

"Any of them look suspicious?"

"Us? No! Just Reveered. It just doesn't feel right."

"And tonight you have AGA at his house?"

"Yes, but I'm not going. I'm protesting."

"How are we going to know who he is?"

"Are you saying I should go?"

"Do you think he's going to kill any of you?"

"Us? Of course not!"

"Maybe we'll come by tonight and ask him a few questions and see how the timelines match up. We follow up every lead."

"Then maybe I should be there to point him out for you."

Deputy nodded to this. He asked a few more questions, took down some contact numbers and asked Judas if she could bring a copy of her church directory.

"I have my prayer one in my Bible, but it's all marked up with request and notes," she opened her big Bible and took out a directory.

"That will do fine," the deputy said.

She handed it to him.

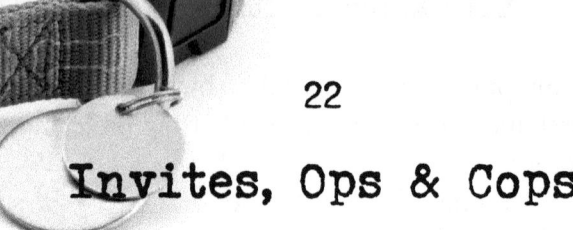

22
Invites, Ops & Cops

One hour after school ended, Suzan Windstop's one true friend, her cat, got sick. It lay still like one of those perfect pets; the battery operated purring furballs that parents buy at the mall during Christmas time. It didn't wake up. With her mom gone and her dad's new cell phone number lost, she did the only thing any broke teenager could do. She wrapped up the cat in a towel and took it to Dr. Carp's.

Spam's teeth had just gotten mashed back in a few hours ago and were pasted into place with something tasting like Nailglue®. Spam opened the door and let Susan in. His jaw was too stiff to talk and his eyes were black. He nodded for her to follow him like a butler would.

"What are you doing here?" Susan asked.

"Sanctuary." His hand gestured to the silver table. "You?"

Susan held up her motionless cat. "How'd you get your teeth back into your mouth?"

"Wow Spam! Dude!" Carp rescued. Or, more accurately, interrupted to protect himself since didn't have a license to practice dentistry on a human.

Susan held out her pet to Carp like it was a homemade apple pie.

The man took it and frowned. He left them and went into the other room.

"He looked upset. I hope it's not expensive," Susan said.

Spam tried to ease her stress. "He juff hates cats."

"You look how I feel," she said. "You must be sick of this town."

"Hmm."

"You wanna come to Sacred Keg with me tonight?"
"Whath's that?"
"A sacred party. I mean, I'm sure it's not *thee* sacred keg, but it's still a party! And who knows?"
"Whath's a farty?"
"It's where you go to have a good time."
"So whath's a bad time?" He unsettled her.
"Not being at a party!" She smiled a row of perfect teeth.
His hurt all the more. "How can use words like good and bad without referring to right and wrong?"
"What's that supposed to mean?"
"It means you prefer sweet talk instead of the voice that will help you face your sin so you can repent."
"You think *I'm* a sinner?"
"I think when it comes to morality, your cat's a lot healthier than you are. And when it comes to righteousness, we all belong in biohazard trashcans. I'm an authority on sin. I killed my family," Spam said.

Carp came around the corner after listening in a bit.

She turned.

Carp was genuinely sad, especially for the girl. "Your pet likely ate rat poison," Carp said. "I don't think its liver is working."

A tear welled in Susan's eye and she went to the man and rested up against him.

He held her hug and gave another confusing look to Spam. "We'll keep the cat here overnight. Who knows? I've already been wrong three times today and it ain't even over yet."

She stood upright, thanked the vet, wiped a tear and looked to Spam. "Good bye Spam. I liked you better when you didn't talk." She turned and walked out and let the door slam.

"Are all the girls at your school like the two pretty puffs here today?"

"Yea. And they can't get enough of me."

Coach called Captain Ron Robertson to meet him an hour before the rest of the team arrived.

"What happened?" He got to the point. "Sit."

Ron sat.

"So?" Coach asked.

"Spam was recruiting again. Taking players from the program."

"Is that why What's-His-Face got suspended?"

"It was going to be him or me. I wanted to kill that kid." Ron searched for words. "Everybody is listening to him, Coach. The players who skipped practice yesterday are missing tonight's game. More have joined. And they want to stand on the sidelines and watch!"

"I thought that was a one day thing!" Coach swore some more.

"There's a connection between Spam…"

"He the one that never speaks?"

"Not anymore. We can't shut him up. There's a connection between what he says and what people do."

Coach swore in denial. "Big Man Frank got a busted arm because Little Boy Spam?"

The captain nodded. "And it ain't no one day thing. It's like he's been brewing this forever. It's like all he wants is to destroy the program. The school. The town!"

"Brewing what?"

"I don't know. I don't get it. But that kid is weird. We kicked the crap out of him coach. And then he just looked at us… well…"

"...Well what?"

"He wasn't afraid."

"But that was before he got his face caved in."

"No. It was after," Ron said. "How do you scare someone off a high horse if they've already fallen off it a thousand times? We knocked his teeth out of his head, coach, and we still can't hurt him! He ain't normal, Coach!"

"Let it go. Be like him and don't take it personal. Now it's time to focus. We need your leadership now more than ever. Now you got bigger opportunities! These murders brought in news crews! And not just TV 8 from Grand Rapids either! The whole nation might hear about you after tonight's game!"

"What?"

"Where have you been? The whole town thinks the game should be cancelled! But the AD won't because he's on our side. We can't forfeit the game and keep our record. We can't reschedule and keep home field advantage. But who cares about that! You're the Tremble High leader the news wants to feature! They don't want the Mayor. Or me. Nobody but you!"

"What are you talking about?" Ron asked.

"CNN and FOX were my office an hour ago. Together! Talk about rivalry! Did you know that?" He lowered his voice and dropped his chin. "I spoke with them. They always want the inside track you know, and people across America may not care about tonight's score. People just want carnage. Just like college coaches!"

Coach nodded to the field so Ron could now see big dishes feeding satellites. "And your voice will speak to the news after the game! It's beyond insurance for your D-1 scholarship! That's done. But now with a name, Ron Robertson, you only do two years of college and then pro! Look at the irony. If you can handle the pressure of playing football when a murderer is circling the field! You can handle D-1 stress. You can handle the NFL! It's perfect! Are you up for it?"

Ron nodded. "Whose here?"

"Tonight the college scouts aren't the only one's listening. A man is here from the Oakland Raiders! The Oakland Raiders! Tonight, win or lose, you will be telling America that Football at Tremble High is a celebration of life! Are you up for THAT?"

Ron slugged his chest. "I'm on it!" He felt the fire.

Coach dropped a hand to Ron's shoulder as his other hand Kung Fu'd the air. "Now, let's go over the basics again when talking with the press!"

Seven days after Deontra was attacked, she knocked on the parsonage door with Sister Sage.

Father Albertson opened the door and heat exhaled from his home. "How are you child? Sister?" he asked.

Deontra stood still, then got nudged by Sister Sage. "I'm afraid," Deontra said.

"Come inside." With the door closed, the three sat in a breakfast nook. "What are you afraid of?" the priest asked. "The boys who hurt you?"

"Not of them. Of Him!"

The priest looked around, then smiled. "Who? The murderer?" That seemed logical. He lost some sleep on that one himself.

"No. *God*. God heard my prayers!" She was whispering. Her voice carried the words with a thin veil that threatened power, danger, violence and justice.

"God hears all our prayers."

Her tone was hushed as the secret uttered out. "Ya. But God *answered* my prayers. *They are dead!*"

"All are dead who do evil. It is through Christ Jesus all can live."

"Father, you don't understand!" Her huge, dark eyes covered her whole face like a Precious Moment figurine as she looked up to him. "The three murdered boys are the one's who attacked me! They met God's Death Angel!"

"Oh dear." He looked at Sister Sage. "That is a problem!"

Sister Sage didn't seem too troubled by the news.

Then something shifted in his mind and ignited his eyes. "And you feel responsible because you prayed?"

"Yup," Deontra nodded.

He smiled from his soul. "Deontra! Deontra! You are sad! You took responsibility. You *have* forgiven them! You *have*!"

She nodded. "Yup. But what about the dead? I don't think God *forgave* them."

"Jesus once told a coward to let the dead bury the dead, but in our case, I think Jesus would want us to go to the police."

The investigation took its first step forward when Deontra Schnidorf, Father Albertson and Sister Sage found Officer Brighton. OOB was at the game with a dozen other cops and held a hand up when they started to explain.

"Wait! I gotta see this!" OOB said.

Tremble was in scoring range. Then fill-in receivers dropped four consecutive perfect passes in the end zone from Robertson.

Eggville got the ball back and killed the clock on downs.

OOB did his cursing and asked for forgiveness in the same breath. Then all four turned and looked at each other as the crowd around them starting flowing the other direction towards the parking lot.

The crowd was stunned and many kicked what they could.

"Now what was it you three wanted?" OOB asked. "Four passes dropped! I'm glad you weren't the Chaplain or you'd be hot water!"

"I know why they are dead!" Deontra said to him and something clicked deep in the cop's mind.

OOB saw the priest confirm and Sister Sage look at her feet and knew that another big break in the case had come to him. He took his shoulder mic and started yelling numbers into it. He smelled a promotion.

Tremble High lost to Eggville High 31-27. Ron stood tall and proud in front of camera lights as dozens of journalists jockeyed for questions. Black grease paint under his eyes was smudged from contact and sweat. FOX asked a question after he pointed to them.

"How are the murders at Tremble affecting the student body?" FOX asked. Strobes flashed off Ron's game face. Cameras rolled tape.

"There's a.... There is a great rivalry between Tremble and Eggville High School. I have a lot of respect for their program and how their coaches prepare the team to put their hearts into every single play. As you know, one third of Tremble's starting players chose to boycott tonight's game to honor the recent unsolved murders of three Tremble High School students. I, and all Tremble mourn these tragedies!" Microphones lifted throughout the crowd. This was good stuff. Some leading edge follow-up questions slipped out but got ignored.

"But," Ron paused, and sparked adrenaline passion in his eyes, "I want America to know that violence and bloodshed is not only a problem in Tremble! Violence and bloodshed is an *American* problem! I for one will stand and salute any and all who gather weekly in the arena of sport and compete against the very few who bring bloodshed and heartache to the streets of America! May a day come when all the world fights on the fields of sport and all violence is conquered!"

Many applauded. A few even whooped it up.

Ron waved. Having said his piece, Ron took coaches advice and walked with purpose through the reporters. They got what they wanted. And moreso. They got what they needed.

On a whim, Ron turned and saw cameras yanked off tripods and stuffed into bags as reporters rushed away. *That was quick*, he thought.

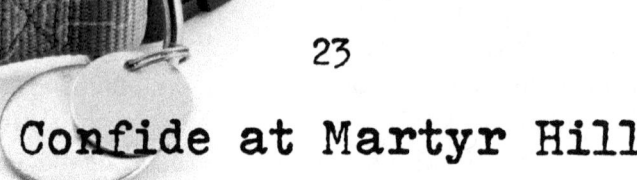

23
Confide at Martyr Hill

Spam looked hard at Carp and saw a nervous man. Their hands and fingers were hard and cold from loading frozen deer. Freezers emptied and leaf springs under the truckbed sagged and complained. Spam closed the gate on the pick-up. It was earlier than usual and Carp seemed rushed.

"What's bothering you Carp?" Spam asked.

"Deer season."

"Why's that?"

"Depends. It's good 'cause I get bones and waste from all the deer processing guys. But guns drive the deer to hunker down and slow up road kill."

"Ain't that when all the bucks move around and get creamed?"

"Yea. But I'm worried about my horde?"

"Ya. Maybe we should ration them out."

"No. It was just a light winter last year and the pups survived."

"That's good. Ain't it?"

"It's eight times the mouths to feed," Carp answered as they got in the truck and started rolling toward Hordeland.

"What's Sacred Keg?" Spam asked.

"You don't need to worry about that."

"That pretty Susan asked me to go."

"Ya. But that was before your little theology beeped her buttons."

"Well. What is it?"

"I don't know."

"That'd be the first. Not your first lie, but the first time you don't know something about Tremble."

"So what your point?"

"What's Sacred Keg?"

Carp gave in. Besides, it was easier to answer this question and avoid talking about what was really under his skin. He looked at Spam. "You see Tremble as a rich town? You see a lot of fancy cars and pricey hobbies?"

"No. Not really. Some farmers get some new tractors once in a while."

"That's to be expected. So who has the money? Parents have mortgages and credit card debt up the butt. Where's the free flowing cash?"

"There isn't any."

"There's money. There's tons of it. Who do you know who can buy anything they want within reason?"

"Dunno. Most everybody I know can. Within reason."

"Right. Cause you're in school. Kids are the only ones who have untraceable chunks of spending money. You tell me. What do kids buy?"

"Dunno. I'm not much of a shopper."

"Right. We're not in the fashion zone you and me. So what do kids buy? What do they do?"

"Dunno."

"That's 'cause you live with me. But what do they buy?"

"Dunno Carp. You tell me! I'm the one asking the question."

"Your age is the only one with discretionary money and time, Spam. You guys can buy up or do whatever you want."

"What's this have to do with Sacred Keg?"

"A while back I had some words with Gene Thompson after I bought some of his Ma's land. Well, he tried to bully me out of town. I've always hated bullies. He knows I'm running wild pets on his. . . I mean my land. He beefed up the fence to our north and east something fierce. Since I've been doing

Friday feeding for decades, I sometimes heard music back on his junk land."

"Is that what's bothering you? Thompson knows you're hoarding pets and he can blow your secret? I thought he hates your guts for stealing his land?"

"It's deeded land, Spam. I never swiped it. I just slipped it. I paid his old lady what she wanted. Ain't my fault that all she wanted was to rub her kid's nose in it!"

"Was that right?"

"It was legal. Back then that was close enough. That was in the days when it was The Man against the hippies. I was a little unstable for a few years and saw his fence as, well, sort of an invitation. I wasn't the pillar of conformity you see before you now."

"Must have been some sight."

"Back then I injuned all around Gene's land. The land he owns now. His land's got some features."

"You're not talking about your land?"

"What would give you that idea?"

"Is Mr. Thompson the leader of Sacred Keg?"

"Spam! With the thinking brain! His old decrepit barn ain't so old or decrepit. It's darn nice. About five, maybe six thousand feet, heated and all. Over the decades there's been a lot going on inside that barn. A lot of parties so to speak."

"He owns Sacred Keg?"

"He owns everything. Got himself an underground cave where he home grows Mr. Blue Smoke. He's got himself an old quiet farmer who does all the work drying and curing the pot. What's the big interest in Sacred Keg? How'd you figure he's connected?"

"Well, I *have* been invited."

"This is Carp, Spam. Ain't I a little too crusty for getting yanked? The girl invited you. But you're talking about

Thompson."

"He attacked me in class because of you. Because of your military record."

"Now it makes sense. There's a lot to attack on that."

"So why does he hate us both?"

"Long story."

"How do you get there?"

"The Keg Barn? It's a couple of clicks beyond the east fence."

"Sounds like I got two invitations!" Spam said.

"I don't know," Carp said. "A few years ago some dogpacks started straying over there and taking down Gene's tasty heifers once in a while."

"I bet that fused the friendship."

"He threatened to take me to court if I didn't pay."

"What'd you do?"

"Well, I never did much like bullies. After I bumped heads with his old farmer out there I got a hunch and wouldn't you know. That old green thumb is a wanted man. So..."

"So you got each other over the barrel. He ain't gonna like it that I know about Sacred Keg."

"Well, that depends on what you do about it. You just need to know that he'll do anything to get at me," Carp said. They went quiet as truck lights ate up gravel road to Carp's two-track. When they rolled to the stop at the gate, Spam looked at Carp.

"You think he's got plans for me?" Spam asked.

"He poisons children for a living, Spam. What do you think? But there are bigger problems here than Mr. Green Jeans. You keep a wary eye on the dogs that aren't glowing their eyes at you."

All heavy hitters were at HQ by the time OOB escorted Deontra down the aisle. Deontra's parents, priest and Sister Sage were the entourage wedding party. But all eyes were on the bride.

Chief Zimmer slapped Officer Brighton on the back. "Two breaks in one day!"

Reporters had sniffed gallow-building tension on their scanners back at the football game and were now posted outside trying to get statements so they could boost ratings. Live feeds were already set up. People were primed. It was money for nothing and every pedestrian got bumped to expert status.

Captain Campbell and Sheriff Harry entered chambers crowded with the girl's support team.

"Anytime you feel uncomfortable and want help or more support let me know. More family? More Sisters? More priests? Anything." Sheriff pointed through glass. He sat a heavy, tired body down. Skin hung loose on his face and his hair was going. Big ears drooped. But at least there was hope that this case wasn't going to kill him.

"We have some great female staff that do this all the time. And we can have a psychiatrist brought here just for you. Your lawyers are welcome, and if you have any information on the murders you have a tremendous amount of rights. Pretty much anything you want."

"I'm good," Deontra said. "Let's just get on with it. You're really the Sheriff? The main Sheriff?"

"Yup," Sheriff Harry said.

Deontra's father nodded to her and scooted back his chair. "I'll be right out that door," he said. "I don't like to re-hash some stuff twice."

Deontra smiled at him. "We're you going?"

"I'm gonna be on the other side of the glass," he looked at the cops. "Just to keep honest people honest." He left.

Harry took over. "So you're here to talk about the murders?"

"I am," Deontra said.

"Okay. Talk about the murders," he nodded and another detective pushed a recorder that activated a microphone in the middle of the large round table.

Deontra's team now included her mother, three nuns and the priest.

The cops had about the same amount. Two female detectives were present. Officer Brighton was there as well as the Tremble Police Chief.

"I was raped one week ago to the hour. Last Friday. I was raped by the Dog Pound."

All paused.

"You go to the hospital? We didn't hear." The Sheriff seemed used to dealing with routine rape.

Is it that common? Deontra thought. "I was cared for by the Sisters of the Faith."

"So medically, a gynecologist or specialist was never consulted?" the lady cop asked.

"They didn't get that far."

"Who are they? How many?" the sheriff wanted facts.

"The Four. The Dog Pound," Deontra said.

Captain looked at the Sheriff.

"When?" Captain asked.

"I left the football game at halftime."

"Where?"

"Where what?"

"Where did they attack?"

"In the field below school. The one between the road and the convent. By the Sisters' house."

"Four boys?" Captain asked. "Not five or three? Four?"

"The Four. The only four. Except now there is only one."

"Mutt." Officer Brighton said, receiving a sharp look from the Sheriff and Captain Campbell.

Deontra nodded.

Chief nodded to Brighton.

Brighton left.

"Where's he going?" Deontra asked.

"Oh, just cop stuff," Chief said.

"What do you mean when you say 'they didn't get that far?'" the lady cop asked.

"Far enough to really hurt me. But not far enough to get me pregnant or pass infection."

"Sure you don't want a counselor here?" Captain Campbell cut in, looking into the mirror.

"My council *is* here," Deontra said.

Captain flushed. "Sorry."

Sheriff took over after shaking his head at him. "What did you do? Did you scream?"

"No."

"Why?"

"I was hit so hard, one of my ribs got cracked. I did go to the doctor for that. I had no breath. No strength."

"How long did it last?"

"Forever. They were on me forever."

Seconds passed by. Many of them. Harry was in no rush to bring horror back. "A minute? Five minutes? A half hour?"

"I don't know."

"Did they finish?" lady cop asked.

"No." Deontra thought. She looked at Sister Sage. "Actually, it seems they were just getting started."

"Why did they stop?" Sheriff asked.

"I don't know. The lights came on and the Sister's were there, calling out."

"Did the perps make any noise?"

"No."
"Did you?"
"No."
"How did the Nuns hear?"

Deontra was stunned that she hadn't thought about it before. She looked at the faces around the table but they were as lost as she was. She closed her eyes and thought back. She felt the dew on grass and mist-filled air. Clothing ripped. Shoes were yanked off. Chirping bugs went quiet and she smelled stale breaths, polluting the freshness of the river that gurgled nearby over shallows. Low clouds shone gray from football field floodlights and then she was crying in the safe arms. She came back to the police station.

The cops sat around and waited. They seemed to be in no rush.

Deontra took a breath and calmed. "God. God told the sisters."

At this the Sheriff looked at Father Albertson, then stood up and went to the door and called out. By now word was out and brown uniformed detectives outnumbered the police. Sheriff Harry explained the events of the interview to three detectives.

"Do the job," he said. "Get Forensics over there ASAP. Hand deliver the report to me the second you're done. Take IBO. Bring thousands of bags. Bag it all!"

He poked his head back in the door and looked at the girl and smiled. "Are you brave enough to go meet them out there when we're done here?"

"Yes."

"Going back to a crime scene is horrible," lady detective said. "It'll all come back."

"I know. I've already been there."

"When?" Sheriff came back and sat.

"Two nights ago."

"In the dark?"

Deontra nodded.

"Why?" Father Albertson asked.

"I've always loved the night. When I can't see far, I hear God's whisper." She looked at her priest. "And yes. I forgave the rapist. I prayed to love them. I went to where they hurt me so God would take me serious. But I don't love them all that great yet."

"There's no rush," Chief said.

"What happened?" Father Albertson asked. The other leaders seemed outclassed.

"To them or to me?"

"To you," the priest waved off the dead.

"I want my hope back." She tried to smile but it didn't come. She knew happy endings come at the end.

"What about them?" Chief asked.

"*That's* why I'm here. The Death Angel of God has come to Tremble. The rapist are dead. All but Mutt. And he'll be next unless my new prayers overpower my old ones!" Deontra said and air seemed to leave the room. Harry put his pen down on the yellow note pad, then looked at the priest. Skin on his face went a shade of purple.

Captain Campbell went to the door and almost opened it, but came back and sat. "You told Officer Brighton this? Is that why he was acting strange?"

"He's pretty strange anyway, but yes, I told him."

"What did you tell Brighton?" Sheriff asked after some silence.

"She told him the short version of what she just told you," Father Alberson said.

Campbell went to the door again and called in another female Detective. "Please escort Deontra to room four and stay with her. She needs to wait there alone with you."

"What about them?" Deontra asked.

"They're staying in here with us for a few minutes."

Deontra looked at them. "That doesn't sound good."

"Can Father Albertson come with me?" Deontra asked.

"No. He'll need to stay with me for a while."

"Sister Sage?"

"No."

"Why do you need them all?"

"More cop stuff," Sheriff said.

"What about my mom and dad?"

"We'll need to see them too," he nodded to the glass. "Especially your dad."

"For how long?"

"We just need them for...I don't know. A while."

"How long?"

"Probably overnight."

"How come?"

"Just until we figure this out."

Deontra was escorted out.

Carp let the truck roll around a corner and its headlights lit up the gate and fence to the left and right. They also found themselves looking on a patrol car with a brown suited deputy leaning against it on the safe side of the gate.

The cop touched the brim of his cowboy hat.

"Oh no," Spam said.

"Relax Spam. It's Weary."

"I know. That's why I said, 'Oh no'."

Weary popped the gate and Carp entered his land then Weary closed it and followed them with his squad car to the pole barn.

Carp saw Spam fidget. "Give him a break. He rescued you didn't he?"

"Ya. But he took me to you. That might not count in everyone's book."

"Got a point there. Well, he's on our side now."

Spam opened the pole barn and Carp's truck pulled in. Weary drove in and the door got closed quick.

Weary and Spam looked at each other and walked up to Carp. Carp generated the lights.

Claws scraped at the door and some hungry dogs started howling.

"We can't talk long," Carp said. "Barking will wake the neighbors."

"Spam. Dr. Carp," Deputy Weary nodded at the two in front of him.

"What brings *you* here?" Spam asked his uncle as if the horde was his personal space.

"How you doing, Spam? Doc patching you up still?"

"That'd be illegal."

"Well, we can't have that now, can we?" he turned back to Carp. "I rattled Gene's cage. He stayed in class like you said. But I lit the fire anyways."

"I bet he loves you more now than ever."

"He's connected. I've been invited to leave. And you're right. He squealed on you. Or someone did. You and Spam are on the hook. They're watching the clinic now. They'll be setting the dragnet for you."

"Won't they track the cop car."

"Might. But it ain't no cop car."

"Thanks for coming. The file help?"

"You bet. Nail in the coffin."

Spam looked at one then to the other. "Who they coming for, uncle? They think Carp killed those boys?"

Weary grunted. "No, they're not that stupid. They're stupider. They think you did."

"Huh?" Spam asked.

"Ralax, Spam, this ain't about you." Weary said as he pulled his pistol, snapped open the cylinder and checked his bullets.

Each deputy looked at the list and then back at the Sheriff who had just finished detailing their instructions. They recognized how he had used the words, sensitive and gentle, about fifteen times. But they knew the drill. It was divide and conquer time. The only thing different was that those in the tank were nuns of the Catholic convent and parents of a beat-up teenage girl.

It was a Hail Mary, but they knew the routine. Beat the bushes was their day and night menu until the killer was caught.

"Remember: Suspect everyone. Incriminate no one. We'll let the evidence do that. Just follow evidence and since we have none, we'll have to start with motivation. So far we got us a young Baptist pastor who plays paintball with teenagers. We got us a burned out Vet who, it appears took in that Spam boy and we got us a room full of Catholics."

Cops looked around at each others faces. They nodded.

"We're dragging the others soon enough, but let's run the Pope Pals first."

They left for the room.

All of Deontra's team was gathered before the Sheriff for a moment.

"You all know better." Sheriff pointed his pen at the priest and his group.

"I beg your pardon?" the priest asked.

"Rape is a felony. Felonies are reported."

"We just reported it. And when she told me of the murders, just over an hour ago, we all gathered and went straight to you."

"I'm talking about the rape!"

"The family wanted privacy. This is a private matter." Mr. Schnidorf said in a stone cold mean way.

He looks guilty enough! a deputy thought.

"The law is clear. Leadership reports felonies."

"I've done more to protect my little girl in the last week than your laws ever will! My daughter wanted privacy and I gave her that! She had a week of peace compared to this circus!" Mr. Schnidorf said. "And as far as your laws? To Hell with your laws!"

The priest looked at his feet.

"Three boys are dead. Did you send them to Hell too?"

"What are you saying?" Deontra's mother asked. "It's sounds like you said we are murderers as well as victims."

"Here's what we're saying. You all are our primary suspects. You have a raped loved one and we have a full morgue. As cops we always look at motive. Do you see where this is going?"

They looked at each other.

"You're also accomplices. You withheld information on a related felony. That's another felony. With that and revenge factor because the girl was sexually assaulted. She tells the sisters in the convent, her priest and her parents and wala! Three of the four Rapist die! And die bad, just for the record. The chicken bones are not in your favor, pardon the voodoo metaphor." Sheriff monologued. "I recommend you all secure lawyers before you say things you shouldn't."

"We don't need lawyers," Deontra's dad said.

"You better hope a jury never hears the time sequencing."

Captain Campbell added.

No one moved. Suspects grew nervous and frustrated.

"You better hope that the Town Council and the voting members of the county never hear how you're incriminating us," Mr. Schnidorf said.

"The town council is the voice of the murdered, not the inconvenienced," Sheriff said. "We're splitting you up as is routine. And we're going over some basic questions. That's nothing new. If you feel you need to lawyer up, we don't blame you. You have that right. Frankly, I'd recommend it."

"Are you telling us that all six of us conspired to murder those animals?" the priest said. "And we did this in such a short time and that we have no remorse? Are you saying that our church can produce six sociopaths and then network three capital crimes and countless others? You must be joking on a non-joking matter."

"Here's what I'm saying. I'm telling you that your lives are on hold for the next 12 hours and if you're innocent? Just remember, it's nothing personal."

City police officer Brighton pulled his cruiser into the gravel, keeping his left tires on the pavement of Forest Ave. The stars hadn't started there march across the sky yet. It was going to be a long night. More arrests were coming tonight! The trees in this area squeezed the roadside and their shapeless shadows leered above Brighton and he stayed next to his car as he paced. Swamp forest had always given him the creeps.

But the news he now had for the teacher was something he didn't want to say over the phone.

Headlights appeared. They came to him and slowed to a stop. The window came down. "Thanks for the call," Mr.

Thompson said, "Spit it out."

"Is this all your land?"

"Mostly. What's on your mind?"

"You're boy Spam's got a motive. A big one. We got true crime. Rape. Last Friday around half time the Dog Pound tried to gang bang Deontra."

"Deontra? One of *my* students?"

"Oh. Sorry about that. Your not supposed to know. But CSC started whole thing. It isn't a random killings, like you said. But it looks like your right on after all! Spam's killing the Dog Pound. He must have got wind of it. She's a Schnidorf. Long history with the church. But you didn't hear this from me."

"I know the family. I just didn't know about the rape."

"Don't tell anyone that. It's under a CSC file and we keep the lid on those pretty tight. You understand?"

"Ya."

"So we got an APB out on Mutt for CSC. He's Peter Mongrel's kid and we're hoping to flush out the old man too. Only we lost him."

"And Spam and Carp?"

"Them too. Just out. We staked out their place. Oh! And get this. I got that thing you wanted. You're right! We don't have that Weary guy on the extended team. Matter of fact, he's not even a cop! He sells insurance down in Kalamazoo. So something is going on. We're looking for him too for impersonating an officer!"

"Good work."

"Hey, you're the one who got us looking in the right direction."

"Anything else?"

"Not really. Eventually, we'll send some cars to pick up one of your neighbors down that-a-ways. The guy who works with kids from Tremble Baptist. Plays paintball with them I guess. A report came in listing him as a possible."

"What's up with that?"

"Dunno. We're just being cautious. We're dragnetting everything. Sheriff is holding the girl's family overnight it looks like. At least until we clear the streets of every suspect! We don't want them getting any lynching ideas."

"Good luck."

"Yea. We're not taking any chances. Anyways," Brighton nodded to Thompson, "I thought I'd keep you in the loop."

Gene Thompson nodded back. He appreciated OOB. He looked at his watch. He had time but the news of Weary is what he feared the most.

Cops have rules.

"Hey Officer!" Gene called OOB back.

"What?"

"You better get over to that crime scene. You got the best feel for what's going on."

OOB nodded a back-at-ya.

24
The Hordeland Hounds & Killdeer's Farm

Deontra was led into the field of her nightmare by lady cop, Detective Chanel. She soon realized Cop Army was already there. Generators powered up huge lights. Back by the road, which bordered Tremble High School property was the police tape. Beyond the edge of yellow ribbon the media frenzy was starting. Deontra saw Cameras atop stepladders and reporters combing their hair and testing equipment. Uplink scopes were extending.

"What's happening to my parents and friends?" Deontra asked female cop.

Detective Chanel was a short woman and her Kevlar didn't ride well. She stood with Deontra. Ahead of them was the convent, behind them, the school. Over a mile of yellow tape sealed the area. "They are under the questions," Chanel said.

"Is that bad?"

"Not if they're innocent."

Deontra stopped walking. "But they're innocent! So why the questions?"

Chanel held up three fingers. "That's why."

"What?"

"Three dead. This is as serious as it gets, Deontra. I'll go the rest of my career without a triple homicide."

"I don't like it. You're holding my parents?"

"Look ahead Deontra. You have enough to worry about here. Back at the station that will all calm down in a few hours. But here? Here it is just beginning."

The Hordeland Hounds & Killdeer's Farm

Pamela danced over, up to, and then alongside Ron. Football war paint was still across the bridge of his nose and under his eyes. He tried to look beyond her and focus on his future in the NFL. But as she rubbed along him, sting of defeat weakened and he let his fingers hold her shoulders then drop and take hold of her. Pamela stared up at him and he nodded back.

Now that he was ready, she led him into the back, smoke-filled room where Watson and Mutt were waiting.

The four of them walked into the night. They left the lights, dancing and john-foolery behind and entered the wood.

Mutt led them downhill on an old deer trail. When the trail ended into the thickest stand of dead pine, he stopped. "He said wait here."

"Who?"

"He has lots of names."

"Then it's true!" Ron said. "There is a soul to Sacred Keg!"

As if the tree was alive, two of its branches came down around Pamela. It griped her tight, twisting into her cheerleading sweater and then they saw white claws curling up her skirt.

Deontra then did a circle. She took in the brown, straw grasses. The moist, earthy smell of dew and mud. The richness of the green grass. It took her back a week. Her mind recalled the last thing she told the Sheriff. *Mutt said he'd kill me if I told.* Turning, her eyes caught the school; it loomed on the hill like a Snoopy's castle. She looked back at the convent. It was an old, two story red house, shaped in a rectangle. Old ivy covered most of it and windows glowed like square eyes behind a well-trimmed beard. Their footsteps followed a narrow pathway that cut through the field. Tall grass brushed against them and Detective Chanel stopped to pull stickers from her pant legs. Midway across the field, Deontra stopped her. "This is it."

Detective Chanel held a hand up to stop the army following her and lifted a clipboard and started detailing the area where Deontra was attacked. She spoke into her shoulder radio and the photographer came.

Other detectives started unrolling an inner circle of yellow tape.

Deontra walked off and picked wildflowers. She answered and pointed at Chanel's questions but offered no more. She saw a shadow of a pine and wondered if that was where Wendell Shyly failed. She looked to the school and the sky beyond and smiled sad. *He really killed three of them!* She thought. She knew she wasn't supposed to feel this way, but it *did* impress her. *Or did God do it through you, Wendell? Did you pray for God's help or are you just a cold as the razor that dug into my palm?*

A Forensic Team, pushing a dozen strong, seemed everywhere. Enough flags and cones were placed to make a motocross track.

Beyond the tall weeds, across the fine trimmed lawn, Sisters were nervous. They peered out from behind windows. They tried to smile as Detective Chanel and Deontra came to them.

The convent got invaded. They introduced themselves. It took a long time for the Sisters to sit. They had a special, timed sequence order and kept standing until Detective Chanel cleared her throat. They then bypassed ritual and dropped. Chanel looked at them as suspects too. "A week from last Friday, you rescued Deontra?"

Three cops stood behind Chanel because their weren't

enough seats.

The Sister's nodded, not trusting the lady cop.

"How did you know Deontra was coming?"

"She comes every Friday." Sister Maria spoke. She was the leader.

Chanel wondered if she could fire a bow-and-arrow. "Who turned the lights on?"

Silence fell.

They looked at each other.

"The lights scared away the dogs! Who turned them on?" Deontra asked.

"They were already on." Chins furled in agreement.

"No they weren't!" Deontra said.

A frail, elderly lady lifted a finger.

"The noise. I was upstairs." The old sister said and all heads turned because she was the Prioress. If she were more humble she would be a pile of clothes on a pair of shoes. This was news and all leaned in. She had more to say.

"I turned the deer lights on," the Prioress repeated. "The flood lights. We call them deer lights, because we use them to watch the deer," she said.

Nuns nodded to this clarification.

"Why did you turn on the lights?" Chanel asked.

"The sound."

Chanel clicked the pen again and brought up a clipboard.

"What sound?" Deontra asked.

"The window. Something nearly broke the window."

"Take me there," Chanel was led upstairs to a reading room facing the forest.

A train of people followed.

"I was sitting right here," the old one pointed to a worn chair as she walked to the window. "There. On the outside. See the dirt?"

Chanel looked at the other deputies. She dropped her chin to her radio, "You boys need to get some lights on the convent. Get them trained up here, right now!"

Two other cops left.

"Where?" The radio asked as Forensics replied.

"Look up." Chanel said and flicked on and off the room light next to the Deer Light Switch.

"Is there a problem?" the old nun asked.

"We're going to need to bring a few more people up here."

Investigators started combing the yard, searching for a stone, stick or projectile that had dirt where it was supposed to be clean. It took 15 minutes to find it. The stone went into a plastic bag and a flag marked where it was discovered. Detectives backed up and looked at the house from the rape scene. The stone was a simple one. Round and smooth. A plain old Michigan stone that spent the better part of its life under water and glacier.

But it was to the left of the window from the attack scene. Investigators lined up the place where the stone was found to the window, and geometried a line from where the stone could have come from.

The line took them away from the rape scene. It seemed to have been thrown from around a pine tree.

Three cops turned and faced the house. "We got us a *peeper*," a deputy said.

"If I threw the stone at the house from here, and hit the window, would it land there?" He pointed at the flag. They backed up a little to the right and finally agreed. The needles under the tree were relatively smooth and neat. They scooped up anything that looked out of the ordinary and stuffed bags for trace.

A group of deputies and police had gathered and were comparing notes under the lights hitting the house by the generator.

Officer Brighton was there. He had just come back from Mutt's house but the boy was gone. OOB now looked at the convent. He saw the ladder where someone was climbing to the window. He thought about Thompson's pep talk and did a circle.

Two nuns were outside, answering questions.

Deontra was on the lawn talking with Deputy Chanel.

Then the eyes of OOB narrowed. Too stunned to speak, he started squeaking. His arm was out and he pointed a finger, stumbling toward the convent across the lawn.

Two men followed his enchantment. They lined up next to him and saw it.

They were looking at a black arrow, jutting out from the ivy, stuck into the brick façade.

The three boys froze, and when it changed from a tree to a human, it got more disturbing.

"It's Deer Face! *He's got me again!*" Pamela announced. "Doctor! Doctor! Gimme the news!" she smiled to Ron. "No boy scouting here tonight, Ron." She was scared and uncomfortable, but she was deadly serious. "Sacred Keg is for keeps! Here we do what *he* says or it only gets worse. I don't want the pressure of Mutt's pasture. I want to have fun! I'm not ready for work. But none of us can do anything until this craziness is done," she lurched in pain as something pinched her from behind.

"You'll kiss away two grand a week for fun?" Mutt asked, exhaling smoke from a roll as if seeing a girl get fondled by a tree was all in a day's work.

Actually it *was* work for Pamela. But she knew she wasn't the first to play kick the keg with the treehugger.

"Let her be! This is all Spam's fault. Don't hurt her!" Ron cursed hard. "It was Spam who turned Ryan on Big Frank. I'm ready to do anything!"

"Then stay there and do nothing for a minute," a man whispered. A bony finger pointed to Watson. "How can I trust you?"

Pamela winced again. "Tell him!"

"Between the cops, murders and Spam, it's only a matter of time before we go down. I for one can't afford any of this. I got plans. We got our tickets!" Watson said.

"Tell him why you hate Spam and let's get this touchy-feely crap over with!" Pamela wiggled and spoke directly to Watson. "He needs to see that your secret is good enough to be on the team."

"What?" Watson asked.

"Tell him!" Pamela said.

"We're the thieves," Watson said to the tree. "Your Spam knows we're rich."

"But you eat junk every lunch!" Mutt barked. "Nice! That's why I can't get a truck, man! Image is innocence."

"We have $32,000 and we leave after Thanksgiving for Australia's surf beaches," Watson said. "We don't come back."

"How's Spam know?" the tree asked.

"You don't know? We used a dead cat to separate Maybell from her money."

"Nice!" Mutt said.

"Go on," the voice nuzzling into Pamela's hair whispered.

"The dead cat ended up at Carp's place. Your place. Ace didn't know. How could he? I don't know how it happened. But Spam got it. He knows."

"Someone dropped it off. OOB took Maybell to see it at the clinic and the pieces came together last Sunday. There was nothing I could do. Spam figured it and told me afterwards.

He's crafty."

"Spam caught you?" Mutt asked.

"At least he didn't kill my friends," Watson reminded Mutt and turned to Deer Face. "He brought that dead cat to school lunch. Before his herd gathered and Ron's theatrics, he gave it to me."

"Sounds tasty," Mutt said.

"He put the bagged cat on our table next to our PB&J and told me to take a peek," Watson said. "I was stunned."

"So?" Pamela asked.

"So he told us to give the money back to Maybell."

"Or else?"

"He didn't say or else. He just told us to give the money back," Watson said. "Who are you really. Are you Carp? Come on, Carp! Where's the love? I can't do that. We're gone soon enough. Won't that do?" He spoke to the deer hide face among the trigs.

"Keep it!" the tree said. "You stole it. It's yours. But two days ago things were perfect. You have to admit, Mutt, we were all getting rich. Now I'm totally exposed. Cops are on me like me on Bam Bam! Spam went protective instinct. And he got Ryan and Sherri to go with him. And the football team! The Dog Pound. Sacred Keg! He's killing us!"

"Coach said the same thing!" Ron said and frowned back at Pamela who seemed content despite being handled.

"My dad says cops'll get me before the weekend. Unless I go subterranean. That's no life! Now this is my last party because of Little Orphan Spammy."

"Wait! You can't be serious." Ron said. "Spam's the killer?"

The monster discarded Pamela into Ron's arms. He stepped into the moonlight, leaving some of his branches behind and forced the three boys to take a step back when they saw the mask. "She's next Ron! Spam's going to kill her too. After Mutt!"

Pamela adjusted herself.

"Mutt, Spam somehow knows of the rape. He's coming for you, but every cop in tri-county is now on his tail and yours too. Watson's too. Keg's too. All because of you, Mutt."

Mutt toed earth.

"Are you ready for the truth, Mutt?" the sunken deer face asked.

Mutt turned to the beast.

"You go and take the rap for the rape."

"What happened is not as bad it sounds!" Mutt said. "But I'll do the time. At least I'll survive."

"And you?" the man looked at Pamela. "Why did you arrange it! For *him*?" the monster pointed to Ron. "You gotta be kidding? He watched me claw you up and just stood there! Some hero!"

"But I told him it was all right!" Pamela said.

"Since when does a hero listen to a maiden?"

"Spam murdering off the dogs is ten times the hero as him. And more deadly than all of us. You might want to start thinking like that in the interest of surviving this week! He knows how to kill!"

The teenagers looked at each other.

"So here's what we're going to do," Deer Face said. "The cops aren't going to arrest Spam tonight. We're going to kill him. Then we're going to make dog food out of him! Then our troubles are behind us."

The three boys looked at each other. "Who are you?" Watson asked.

"You all trusted me, so I'll trust you so it's sacred. I'm you new cash source! The Rex Vet Rx of the Free World! I'm Sacred Keg! The Forest King. I'm the Vietnam Veterinarian! Now that we all know each others secrets, we all are in the

The Hordeland Hounds & Killdeer's Farm

pact."

Pamela looked at the man. *Man! Mr. Thompson can lie like you read about!*

Ron nodded. It was all coming together. His season might still be saved!

"Mutt," a white, deer-rib claw pointed at him. "You take Bam Bam over to where those church burps are playing paintball. I'll follow. Susan will make sure Spam gets there. We'll put Spam down once and for all. It's gotta be done. It's the humane thing to do."

Mutt nodded. The plan had already been explained to him. He didn't know why or how the killer would be there and he didn't care. He knew where the rope was. He had seen hangman's tree. And he was feeling good. The hunted was a hunter once again.

"Ron," a claw pointed. "You and Watson go back to the party. It's still Sacred Keg and we've a reputation to protect! Look there," he pointed. "Can you make out the trail?"

Ron looked at them. "For the record, I just heard that we're trying to catch the killer! Not kill the killer."

"You got it! But if something goes wrong, you have nothing to hide. I trust you to tell the camera's the way it is. With your own style. You can still win this season!"

Ron nodded and looked at Watson. When they turned back, there were only four teenagers in the woods.

"Where did he go?" Ron asked.

"Don't ask," Pamela said. "He'll hear. And make sure Carp doesn't ever do that to me again!"

Ron nodded to his girl. *Spam was right. I am a coward. But even Passivites don't want to see their girls get racked over by a nasty Vietnam Veterinarian.*

25
The Posse & the Piper

Wendell continued to role over the rhythmic bumps in the sidewalk. He felt like a hungry rodent in a clear tunnel. The little football game was long over. He had listened to little Ron Robertson, Bam Bam's little boy toy, make his little speech to the little press.

Afterwards, as he biked towards home, he saw the cops crawling all over Rape Field. *Good for you, Deontra! You got the cops after Mutt!* A sickened feeling came to his stomach. There was no way to get to Mutt in time now. The cops would get him first. He thought of Bam Bam. He had a lot more thinking to do on her. Killing a scum mutt was one thing. Murdering a cheerleading captain was another. Yet she was the one who told Mutt where to lift his leg. She had it coming.

Wendell biked. He had too much to do and too little time. He knew he could kill Pamela. Especially if he had the weekend to soak himself in hate. *I can go deeper,* he thought. *I can hate more than last week. I can kill harder and darker.*

He made it home, parked and locked his bike and entered his house. He didn't know why, but somehow felt that there must be a way to torture Pamela for a long time.

"Who won?" his father asked, hitting the Mute Button on the remote control. His face glowed blue, the TV being the only light.

"What?"

"Who won the game?"

"We lost."

"What happened? That fancy quarterback get hurt?"

"No. Most the team didn't dress because of those murders," Wendell said.

"What?"

"Ya."

"How many wimped out?"

"Dunno. Maybe a third of the team." Wendell spoke smooth and clear, not a ripple or hesitation. He was getting good. "Ma, can you drive me to AGA?"

"RBY is still on? Oh that's great. That's really great! You making new friends?"

"Some. I like Reveered."

"I don't," Mr. Shyly said. "And I'm not the only one. You keep an eye on him for me."

"Sure. Whatever," Wendell said.

Mrs. Shyly pulled the keys to her minivan out of her purse and Wendell followed. When they made it to Reveered's driveway she looked around. "Where is everyone?"

Wendell sprung the handle and stepped out. "Thanks. They're around back." He turned to leave.

"Wendell," she called out.

He caught the door as it was closing and opened it back up. He put his face in the opening. "What?"

"I'm proud of you for coming. This is a tough time and I'm proud that you're turning to God during all this killing."

"It'll be over soon enough," he said, closed the door and turned away. Once Bam Bam and Mutt were gone, he'd be proud of himself too. Rounding Reveered's house, he saw the fire up on the hill and a group by it. *Angie's group of mourners, no doubt.*

AGA had already started. Holy War made perfect sense to Wendell. It seemed to be his type of game. Only he didn't understand why Reveered gave the Martyr Team a gun.

"Why do you give us a gun?" Wendell had asked Reveered at EPBM.

"The team is all boys." Reveered had said.

"Why a gun?"

"All boy's like guns. There's no better way to tempt a Christian than with a gun. It makes turning your cheek nearly impossible."

"It does," Luke had agreed. "We know we shouldn't kill, but we always want to shoot people who hurt us. Especially Angie."

Wendell remembered how the group had looked yesterday. They were as scared as he was on Monday.

Reveered had seemed to have felt Wendell's discomfort at EPBM about AGA Holy War. "Do you have a problem with guns or with Holy War in general?" Reveered had asked.

"I'm good with it." Wendell said, not have problems with war. "I just never liked guns I guess."

Reveered had jumped and rushed to Wendell and put one hand under his chin and the other on his curly hair like a TV Faith Healer. "Demons be gone!" Reveered had started yelling. "Restore this currupt young boy to American status once again! May he love guns! Return him to his former glory!" Reveered kept his hands on Wendell and faked the exorcism.

Wendell now smiled. He remembered how everyone had laughed. It was too bad Angie had already left.

He now watched a martyr slump off from the group and climb the hill. Soon the music, lyric and tune filled night air. Above the trees, shadow seemed to whisper as it blocked the stars and turned the ground to black.

Boys scattered.

Girls grouped.

In the confusion, Wendell got separated from both and walked to the top of the hill by the martyr who was staring at some boycotters at the fire.

For some reason, Wendell turned back and looked

towards Tremble.

The road coming from town sparkled in red and blue cop strobes.

They had found him. He looked around and saw the martyr facing away from him, singing like a bird and probably blinded to the darkness from staring at the fire.

Wendell slipped up close and took hold of the tree and climbed up.

It was a good thick-branched oak that had enough leaves to hide a small aircraft. Whatever. He was too tired to run. He made it up into the thicket, settled and listened to Jesus Freak music get blurred over with sirens.

26
Martyr Hill Madness

Deputy Weary dialed his phone. It cast a blue glow on some weeds and a nearby tree.

Spam and Carp heard it ring and a woman's voice cut in.

"Hello," she said.

"Maybell King?"

"Yes."

"This is Deputy Weary. We spoke earlier."

"You got the location?"

"Carpland. West entrance."

"Where you described?"

"Yes."

"They'll be there!"

Weary flipped the phone shut.

"Who's coming?" Spam asked.

"A posse," Weary said.

"What?"

"Maybell King's four football captains. We can't trust anyone else."

"Why do we need them?" Spam asked.

"How long's Thompson been teaching Government?" Weary asked.

"Dunno."

"How about thirty-one years! Long enough to corrupt the entire law enforcement of the county. By comparison, this county isn't eighty percent down on drug arrest because it's good. It's down because it's dirty. Maybell's four boys will balance the odds. They'll be like The Four Horsemen of The

Apocalypse."

They got in Carp's truck and went to meet them.

The horsemen arrived. Spam swung open the gate and they drove by him in a SUV.

Weary spoke to them as Carp and Spam waited in the truck. Then the deputy came to the truck and got in. "Let's go."

Carp drove Spam and Deputy Weary to an old tree in the middle of a shrubby field and Spam hustled out and attached the truckbed rope to the tree and then jumped into the truck as the hungry horde circled.

Deputy Weary looked at the horde swarm the deer piled in the truck, then he turned to Carp. "Carp you're sick, there's upward towards a thousand!"

Dogs of all shapes began circling. They were medium size and bigger. The weak never fared long on Carpland.

Carp drove away, the rope tied to the bottom deer in the back to the truckbed tightened. The knots held and the entire 2,000 lb. pile of venison slid off the truckbed onto the ground. "That'll keep them going for a while," Carp said.

Weary looked back. A dog pile of biblical proportions developed. "Carp, you need some serious psychological help," he said.

Carp grinned.

Spam nodded.

The SUV followed them to the pole barn where they loaded Spam's ATV into the truckbed.

Then they drove south to the stump line that hid the chain link fence from outsiders.

Spam bounced out the ATV in the middle of some field and hurried back into the truck.

Carp now drove east a good ways, then he killed his lights and the SUV did too. Both vehicles rolled along by starlight, then they stopped and got out.

Out of a circle of men, Carp spoke to Spam. "You sure?"

Spam nodded and they all crossed the last two hundred yards on foot until they came to the east property fence and the massive stump-pile lines beyond it.

Concerned about the horde, they looked behind them most of the time. They found a crude gate and left Carpland and began their trespass. Carp and Weary dunned nightvision and Spam followed, trying not to fall or trip. Behind Spam came the posse. They walked without caring much about sound or what they crunched underfoot. They were on a mission.

As the posse trooped on, each seemed to find a good stick that had a strong root system. They kept swapping them out until they had themselves four good clubs.

Soon the night sounds of the forest weakened. Swamp frogs stopped creaking, the hushing of leaves stopped and the grate of branches grew softer. Even the stomping footfalls of Maybell's henchmen seemed quieter.

Music now drowned out the forest whispers and then a barn appeared. Dark damp woods showed bright against black, lifeless windows. Empty for decades.

"What's this?" A horseman asked, pointing with a club.

But the barn pulsed.

"Sacred Keg!" Weary said. "Now your speaking my language!"

Their eyes adjusted and parked cars, shining in dew appeared in a far off clearing.

Spam's guts felt sound bass and he walked forward and stood at the edge of the treeline ahead of Weary and Carp. Spam blinked away the night and studied the roof sag and warped planks.

"The century old barn is but a shell," Carp whispered. "Inside is another building, insulated and warm, blending old and new."

Weary lifted his nightvision. All the low branches around them stuck out like the arms of nymphs that want to grab and eat children. Their breath stayed white and hung around them as if the area didn't need help in making fog. Weary lowered his vision and his eyes shined starlight as they opened to Spam. "Why are you doing this again?" he asked

"Suzan asked me to help her," Spam said.

"I didn't hear that," Carp said.

"Neither did she."

"You know what happens when boys lose their girls?" a man asked.

"I grew up among animals," Spam said.

"People are worse. They're not fixed you know. You're forbidden to be here aren't you?" Weary asked.

"Forbids only come from God. But I *am* intolerant to what Suzan tolerates and that's bound to cause some issues."

"You're walking on water when you go inside. You lose your focus and they'll drown you like a witch," Carp said.

"Evil is not overcome by passive people, Carp. And true witches can't be drowned." Spam turned to him. "When God cut into my life, Carp, there went my life. I don't care what happens in there tonight. I really don't. I just care that I go. That I stand. That I ask Susan to leave and whoever else to leave. Actions in heaven have already determined what will happen in there."

Spam faced the barn and started walking.

The men watched Spam cross the dark lawn and stand next to a door. Then they saw a beam of light flash out, a blast of sound and then all went dark and quieter.

Spam had entered Sacred Keg.

It's only a few minutes back to the clinic, Carp thought. *Any bumps or bruises I can fix there.*

Weary held still. He knew different. He knew this was the realm of monsters.

The posse came alongside him, clubs up.

Carp drifted back into the forest, pulling another set of headgear from his pack. He put the helmet on, pulled off his boots and went sockfeet into the thicket. Before him was a world of colors, mainly of blackish blue and dark green except for the two rabbits that were hiding over fifty yards to his left. They shone red. Behold the power of infrared technology.

Inside the barn, Spam saw no one. It was pretty dark, but he felt the driving music. His eyes adjusted to low light. He smelled woodsmoke and noticed a wood burner in the corner under a smokestack. For a moment he thought he was alone, then his eyes focused on the grouping. Bodies layered one area like snakes in cold pits. Spam's heart cooled at their perversion. He pulled the power cord and music died.

They turned from each other and stared at Spam. By now the rumors had been whispered and they looked at the Dog Pound Killer.

Spam walked toward them; something stirred within. He wasn't sure if he was getting stronger or weaker, angrier or sadder, but he kept walking. He saw teenagers but they were no longer young. Maybe they hadn't been for years. "Stop," he said. His voice was soft and low. Almost indifferent.

Their withering slowed.

Spam took a step. "You're all human here. Where's your guilt? Are you living by rules you made up yourselves?" Spam asked the question in a flat, tired voice.

Seven young men and a dozen girls looked dumbfounded. Some opaque eyes never even blinked. Others seemed unable to understand Spam, but he spoke on, despite teeth pain from Carp's dentistry and a sample dose of canine pain killers.

Girls giggled as Spam stepped closer and a few long, slender arms reached for him to join.

"Behavior like this *is* forbidden by God. Such evil will torture those who it possesses." Spam stepped closer.

A few boys took offense and squared their shoulders at him. Their hands buried in tangle of long hair of girls.

"Spam! There's only one way you're going to be leaving Tremble. And that's in cuffs to prison where other murderers will feast on you!" A boy yelled.

But everyone else held still and did nothing. They were the insiders. Their scoop fingered him as the killer and they were nervous about being in the presence of the murderer.

Spam closed the distance and stood at the threshold of red light haven. "You're not deaf to my words." Spam pointed to Suzan. "Rise up and follow me out, Susan. Run away from this mess!"

No one moved until a small girl struggled in a violent way with persons next to her. Everyone looked at her. Two boys held her tight. Her hand went numb from being squeezed. But in a moment of power, she broke free and ran behind the boy called Spam.

Two more girls followed and huddled together behind Spam. Their fingers groping floor, searching for clothes.

Suzan Windstop looked at Spam but was trapped, she was struggling to leave the center grouping but she was afraid.

"Let her go." Spam spoke to them.

They did.

Spam's utterness disturbed them. Being seen as a killer started to mean something. His being there created the magic of the message.

Susan rose at once and walked to Spam, using her long, slender legs to step over bodies under blankets. At the edge she yanked one blanket, then another.

Spam put his hand on the small of her back and pushed her behind him.

No one argued.

"Spam," Susan whispered.

"Get dressed," Spam said.

A small, side door slammed open and Ron appeared. "What happened to the music?" Then he saw Spam and his face pruned. "You're not wanted here!" He yelled.

"I know. I am wanted to respect God," Spam said. "You are too. Come with us. Tell God you're done with cowardliness and passivity. Send Bam Bam to Hell."

"You say her name!" Ron swore at Spam in harsh, bitter, cruel terms.

Spam looked at every person in the group. "Who else will follow me out? Follow the ways of God and leave this grave?"

Red faced, Ron stepped forward and walked up to Spam. Veins in Ron's neck surged and his eyes were liquid rage. With both hands he reached out and took Spam by the neck and lifted him clean off the ground. He had caught the killer. *Loser that!*

Spam neither kicked nor struggled as his tongue was squeezed out by Ron's grip.

But Ron forgot what he was going to say because a knife clicked open before his face. He lowered Spam to the ground like Sylvester would Tweety when faced with Grandma's broom.

A very strong thumb had snapped open a long, curved blade of a Spyderco Catherman®. Stainless steal glowed silver in the soft light. It was marketed as fishing knife, but it also seemed to have been created to kill. The weapon had

Martyr Hill Madness 237

come into view from over Ron's right shoulder and now hovered near his face and neck. Knuckles over the handle were near Spam, but the point aimed at Ron, ready for the piercing. The knife deflated the quarterback's ego.

Many had seen what Ryan did barehanded as he maimed the counties largest football player. If they needed a reminder, ironically, they only had to turn. Big Frank was parked by Sacred Keg, palming a pitcher with his good hand.

No girls felt like kissing *him* tonight.

The knife stayed on Ron, then twitched at a girl huddling behind him. "Can Sherri and I come?" Ryan asked Spam.

"I'm not afraid of you Knack," Ron said. "And if you didn't have the drop on me I'd charge you the special night time rate for what you did to Frank."

"But you *are* afraid of me, Captain," Ryan said and no one argued.

Into this mess Spam spoke. "Ryan, only God should kill or use power to wake a heart. To come with life you must leave the death knife."

"Fancy words for a killer!" Ron said.

Spam looked through Ron as if he wasn't there and Ryan obeyed. Many inhaled as Ryan folded the knife and handed it to Ron.

Sherri quickly came to Ryan and took hold of his left arm. Two girls shared a blanket and Susan pulled on some guy's a sweatshirt. She made it look good.

Spam turned to the ones behind him. "Follow me."

The knife clicked open. The group froze.

Ron palmed it easy enough, for the graphite handle allowed good control over the long, curved blade. Ron took a step to Ryan.

From the corner came Big Frank, his thick right hand still clamped his pitcher. His left hung suspended in an air sling with some ice because swelling had postponed surgery.

"Not this way, Ron," Watson said from the pile.

The knife came closer to Ryan.

Spam wondered if Carp had enough stitches in his clinic to knit a slice from such a blade.

"Do it!" Frank yelled.

Ryan just faced the blade. The knife came closer to Ryan's eyes.

Sherri removed her hands from Ryan's left arm when the blade was but inches away.

Watson blended in with the wall and marked the exits. He was down the ladder from Ron and guilt from association with Ryan was going to ruin him.

Freed from Sherri's grasp, Ryan's left arm shot out and his hand clamped on Ron's thick wrist. Ryan's grip had the form of one setting a volleyball.

Now everyone in that room had seen Ron flick a football 60 yards with that wrist, but with a power twist, Ryan just bent Ron's arm, oddly outward and caused the boy to grunt.

The knife popped loose into Ryan's right palm. His fingers clipped it shut, recoiled and popped the blunt graphite into Ron's forehead. Ryan sent Ron to his haunches and opened a small trickle of blood from a Harry Potter forehead cut.

Ryan then flipped the knife into the air, caught it, clicked it open and threw it. It stuck deep in old barn floor with a sharp thewp next to Ron's right hand. It could have ended a career.

"Wanna try that again?" Ryan asked.

Ron slid back as if the knife was a bomb.

"Who else will follow me and leave violence and sin behind?" Spam asked Pamela as she took a knee by Ron.

"Go on outta here!" Pamela raged. "You're hated here!" She reached down to help Ron but he slapped her hand away.

"How long has the smell of this place stirred your heart to hate what is right?" Spam asked them. "Ron! Leave with me. Be free once again. Bam Bams live in places like this. Burn her to the ground and stop feeding the memory." He tossed him a book of matches.

Possessed beyond hate, two other boys lunged to a center beam. One pulled off a metal tool and hurled it at Spam. The rotation of the projectile sheered hair off his head as it whizzed by and dashed Susan's cheek. It hit blunt, but still laid it open.

Susan's hand went to it and blood flowed between her fingers.

Spam turned to Susan and handed her a folded bandana from his pocket. "Get used to pain when you follow God. We broke life so bad, I sometimes doubt if any of it can be fixed this side of heaven."

She covered the wound and nodded to him.

"Get outta here!" another girl yelled.

Frank threw his beer pitcher at the group, clunking it off Spam's head and spraying others in draft.

Even Watson stepped up and waved for them to leave.

Foreigners, who just lost Susan and three other girls, started throwing anything at hand and yelling awful words. Two of them were Nester's and nailed Spam with a chunk of wood. They flapped five and seemed proud enough.

True to form, Spam didn't flinch as he grunted off blows. Then he turned and nodded to the disciples. "Now we leave. Leave this life of sin." Spam slid open the main barn door, throwing light across the night grass.

The pilgrims left the building.

27
Barn Burner

The march to Reveered's land was slow going, but invites were invites, and Spam headed south and out of the forest. By the time they reached the thick brushlands, they were a torn up, half naked and cold group of travelers. Spam hoped Luke was sincere about his welcome but doubted his extras would go unnoticed. He found the southeast game trails that circled Carpland. They trudged on.

"Are you the killer?" Ryan asked during a pause.

"Do I act like one?" Spam asked.

"We're not alone in the woods," Susan said. "He knows were going for Martyr Hill."

"Who?" a girl asked.

Susan looked at them and they lowered their eyes.

"How does he know?" Spam asked Susan.

"I told him," she said. "I thought you were the killer."

"Really?" Spam asked.

She didn't answer as Spam looked at her face. Her hand was red and her fingers were dark. Her blond hair glowed in moonlight and she looked like a postmodern angel with a tragic flaw. She shook her hand and he smiled and nodded.

"It's not far now," Ryan said.

They were on the move again.

Ryan had an arm around Sherri and practically carried one of Susan's friends who had taken a thorn deep into her foot.

Susan's wound had dried some, but she was very pale. The two others trudged on under their blanket.

Spam then turned east until he found the creek that flowed out of Reveered's land. Here they rested, soaking the thorn-stuck foot in icy water.

Susan opened a phone and started working the thorn out.

"Put out the light," Ryan said, looking back into the darkness to the north. His face was smeared with sweat, wood grease and scraped from branches and vine. "Something is out there alright," he whispered.

Sherri heard and cupped the face of Susan's phone until the glow blinked out.

Spam looked to Carpland but said nothing. The horde couldn't breach the fence. If hunger kept them penned, nothing could get them out. "What is it?"

"I hate coyotes," a girl said, hearing some cackles.

"Someone is out there," Ryan whispered to Spam only.

Deputy Weary and the posse each took a barn door. He was now at Sacred Keg and he was going to leave *his* mark on this place. What more could they do to him?

The men burst in. One found the lights. Weary shot the stereo, letting gunfire settle everyone right down. He had raided parties before and set the cockroaches running, but now they had another task.

The posse had photos of each thief. They circled the party elite. Clubs held shoulder high.

Deputy Weary stared at his former police car. Getting it stolen had gotten him thrown off the Tremble Police Force. He turned from it, eyeing the barn. He took in the old iron farm tools hanging on the walls and a huge, turn-of-the-century circular saw blade hanging behind a long strap.

He went to the large, wooden barrel that housed Sacred Keg. He stepped up on the wagon and kicked it over, the metal keg and ice poured out. It was just like his sister had described.

"You, One-Arm Bandit!" his revolver pointed at Big Frank. "Set that big barrel back up!"

Frank one-handed it upright, staring at the keg on the floor and muttering something about alcohol abuse.

"Now dump those bags in. Fill it up!"

A boy tried a dash for the door and took the blunt end of a club in the guts. He went down and was kicked back.

Two posse men had found Watson and were looking for more. They had Watson on a leash against the wall.

Frank and two others finished dumping the last two 100 lb. bags into the barrel. It sat upright by the cop car and was now full to the brim.

He saw feet print on his patrol car and it boiled his blood. *Framing me had been an inside job! And they've been using it for a dance floor!*

A horseman dragged in a hose from the farm diesel tank outside. It gushed. He handed the hose to Weary.

Weary stuffed the pink fuel flow into the barrel of fertilizer. He looked out over the puddle of twenty odd teenagers and waved the gun at all of them. "Where's Thompson?" he asked.

They said nothing. Maybe they didn't know.

Weary doubted that. "You got what you need?" He asked the posse.

They nodded, pointing a club at the bound Watson.

"This here is diesel fuel mixing with Thompson drug fertilizer. Any of you know what fertilizer is made of?"

Some shook their heads. A girl with smeared lipstick seemed bored.

"It's made from Ammonium Nitrate!" Weary said. "With diesel all the basic ingredients come together. Have you ever heard of the Oklahoma City bombing?"

No one moved.

"Ever heard of Oklahoma?"

Barn Burner

Same response.

"Of course not," Weary said. He pointed his gun back at the barrel. "One more question. Have you ever heard of a bomb? Because you will remember this!" he pulled out a red stick that looked like dynamite.

"I want to know where Gene Thompson is!"

No one moved, but the one girl didn't look as bored.

Deputy Weary reached down and twisted off the head of the flare, struck the gunpowder with the rough end of the cap and a bright, red, chemical flame ignited! "I'm willing to die to find Gene Thompson!" Weary said.

No one doubted him here.

The riders of the posse took hold of their capture and stepped toward the door. The diesel was pouring into the granular pellets inside the barrel and mixing.

"I'll help if you let them go!" a boy called out. His face glowed red in the flare light.

"What's your name?" Weary asked.

The party elite in the middle of the floor squirmed.

The posse and their prisoner took another step to the door.

Flame from the flare sparkled down and had now ignited fuel below the keg and fire was creeping up the side of the huge wooden barrel.

"Ron Robertson. I'm captain of the football team!"

Weary pointed his weapon at Big Frank. "You better open that barn door and clear on out."

Frank opened it and cold night air poured in.

"Wait!" Weary called out.

They stopped and turned.

"Safe distance from this blast is over two hundred yards. Don't go for your cars! They are in the radius. Run for the woods. Now go!"

The exodus flooded past him to safety!

Weary trained his weapon on Ron Robertson. "You and me," he said.

The posse left with their hostage.

Weary added the last ingredients to his barrel, looked around at Ron and nodded. "It's happening." He stuck the flare in the top and they ran from the barn.

Acknowledging Ryan's insight that they were being followed, Spam nodded. He knew Carp was sneaking around out there. But he said nothing of the others.

"Where are we going?" a girl asked. "I mean, Martyr Hill doesn't sound like our best chance for survival."

"The Baptist church teenagers meet upstream on Friday nights," Spam said. "They meet on land owned by their pastor called, Reveered. Susan and Ryan were there yesterday. I was invited to come after lunch today."

"You were there last night?" a girl asked Susan.

"What about us?" Sherri asked.

"We got to go," Susan said, looking into the forest.

"We're moving out," Ryan said. "We can't stay here."

"It's upstream a bit," Spam said.

"Is that your plan? Just walk into AGA with us dressed like this. Or undressed like this?" Susan asked.

"Yes," Spam said.

In the forest behind them, an acorn fell from the top of a tree, bounced its way down through branches, then splashed in the leaves on the forest floor. All seven of them looked into the darkness at the sound.

Ryan turned back to the group. "The creek bed is gravel. If we open our phones we can make better time through the holes and over the logs."

Spam nodded. He knew Uncle Weary was after Thompson and he knew Weary wanted to catch him in the unpoliceman sort of way. And Thompson wanted Carp. And that Posse wanted Watson dead or alive. And he knew Mutt and his wanted father were in the mix and both likely believed that he was the killer. As to the barn? He felt that his uncle had some plans for that too.

Spam nodded for Ryan to leave Sherri. They stepped a few paces away from the creek and the girls.

"Whose out there?" Ryan asked.

"Many," Spam said. "Did you see Thompson inside the barn?"

"Who?"

"Mr. Thompson?"

"I've never seen him outside of school," Ryan said.

Sherri came up to them. Her blond hair showed bright in the night. "I know," she said.

"Know what?" Ryan asked.

Sherri looked at Spam. "He wears a deer mask. And has white claws. But it's him."

"Who?"

"Some said tonight that it was that Freak, Carp," a girl said and lowered her eyes.

Ryan looked at Spam. "Around the barn is a masked man. He has bone claws on his fingers. He wants to look scary, that's all. He wears a twisted deer face mask to give the girls a little scare."

"He doesn't ever go in the barn?" Spam asked.

Sherri looked at her feet.

Ryan shook his head.

"What's he do, Sherri?" Spam asked.

By now the other girls had left the creek and circled the boys.

"He sometimes sends for us," Susan said and lifted her sweat shirt, showing her midriff and fresh lines that had been raked across her. "It's a Sacred Keg thing, that's all."

Two other girls nodded.

Sherri looked at her feet.

Spam looked at Ryan and remembered his uncle's caution about predators losing their prey.

"And they said Dr. Carp does this?" Spam asked. "Because he gets the deer road kill from all the car crashes?"

They nodded.

"What do you say, Susan? You saw Carp today. Is it him?"

"No. The rumor started only tonight. Decades of no one caring until tonight? And now all of a sudden it's Carp? It's not him."

"I think the beast is Mr. Thompson," Sherri said and could not look at Ryan.

"Hold up your phones!" Ryan asked the girls.

Two did.

"Spam, you take the lead!" Ryan gave Spam his phone which had a flashlight on it of all things. "Now go! We gotta go fast."

The small group took to the water. Feet soon numbed and they rushed upstream in phone light. Around them was a complete wall of dense swamp brush and darkness, but for jutting tree limbs that tried to hook the blankets over the shoulders of the non-clad girls.

Ryan watched behind, his eyes well-adjusted. Speed was very important.

Deep into the forest of the night, behind a very large tree Deputy Weary stopped and braced himself. He nodded to Ron to be ready.

A few hundred yards beyond the barn in the other direction, four adult men stood in front of Watson. They each held a club.

Watson fought to breathe as the rope dug into his neck and circled the tree behind him. His hands were tied behind the tree too. The rope on his neck was choking him, but it was the talk of the four men that had his attention.

"But he said he would give the money back," a man said. "I can trust you to do that, right?" he looked at Watson.

Watson nodded for his life.

"But he scared mom, scared her good," another said. He was the one who had already thunked Watson a couple of times with the club, starting a trickle of blood that now covered half of the boy's face. "It ain't good to scare Ma. I say we beat him. And beat him good. A boy will remember a good beating his entire life."

Watson shook his head. He wanted to speak, but the last time he had said something, they shoved a farm rag deep into his mouth. Snot and mucous now covered his upper lip because his nose had been clogged.

"We can kill him right here!" a third said. "If we are going to kill him, we should do it here then throw him back in the barn."

At this they paused. "Can't," one said. "It'll blow any second."

"We still have time." They unified on this thought. One looked at his watch.

"Wait," the fourth said. "They'll find the charred body, then it'll be Weary who might get slapped with murder. Let's just beat him to death right here and then do the hole in the ground thing." He spoke and Watson saw that he was holding a old shovel he had taken from the barn.

"But he said he'd give the money back," the first man said.

"The cops for him!" the third said. "Get him on the record books. Wreck his life. They'll get the money. Arrest his cronies and Ma will have respect."

"Weary says all the cops are crocked. They'll keep the money and give back only some. And some rich lawyer will come after us for roughing up a minor."

"Are you a minor?"

Watson nodded, assuring them that his was as minor as minor could be.

"Would you come after us?" the second one asked, jamming the club into the boy's face.

Watson shook his head.

"You promise us you'll give Ma back her money. All twelve thousand dollars or whatever?"

Watson nodded.

Mutt and Pamela dogged Spam's group, but they couldn't catch them in the darkness. First, they expected only Spam. Ahead of them were at least five. And one of them was Ryan which demotivated Mutt. And third, Spam might be small, but he had just killed Mutt's three tough friends deader than Joseph Stalin. Also, Pamela was no woodsman and Mutt knew she couldn't survive the forest without help. When they made it to the stream, he found himself carrying her upstream to where Green Gene said the church burps gathered.

Mutt stopped and lowered Pamela at the edge of Thompson's property where a line of massive trees jutted out rusted wire from their trunks. He lifted a phone to his ear because the area ahead was on fire with cops.

Atop the hill, far away, was a lone tree. To its left was a white house beyond a lawn. Both sides of the creek were landscaped and now swarmed with people and cops. It was civilization.

"Wait where you're at," Thompson's voice on the phone said. "This is too perfect!"

Huddled around the base of Martyr Tree on the turf called Execution Ground, all Holy War patrons had been herded. Dozens of flashlights beamed into their faces and many AGA members held hands to their eyes to shield them from the lights.

Behind the flashlights, a lot of cops from the police and sheriff departments paced as they surveyed the crowd.

Captain Campbell stepped forward after all the AGA group had been accounted for. "Henry Witherbean?" he called out.

No one in the pool moved. A few girl's, one in particular, looked at the lone adult in the crowd and nodded to him for the cops.

The man was covered in military grease paint and full camouflage. At his feet was a high tech paintball gun. The description fit.

The Captain called out again, "Henry Witherbean. AKA Reveered, I am Captain Campbell of the Sheriff's Department."

The man in camo stood up. "I am he," Reveered said.

"Come out of the group!" the Captain said. "We're going to do this peaceful-like!" More than one cop had a hand near their service sidearms.

Reveered came out.

OOB rushed up to the Captain pulled him back a bit and whispered in his ear. "I'm telling you. That right there is Spam. Next to those blanket bombs!"

"Joshua Spamp!" Captain Campbell called out. "Come

forward too."

Spam stood and came out of the group.

Other cops with guns took him and brought him next to Reveered. The two stood as guns circled them. The clicking of handcuffs was heard by all as the two of them were procedured.

Captain Campbell stepped up to the two cuffed persons. "Henry Witherbean. AKA Reveered. And Joshua Spamp. AKA Spam. You are both under arrest for conspiring to murder and for the murders of Stanford Strings, Tommy Smith and Fran Parkington! You have the right to remain silent. You have the right to have an attorney present during questioning. If you cannot appoint an attorney, one will be provided by a court of law!"

Mrs. Witherbean, face flared and flushed, rushed up to her husband. "See! See where this has gotten you? Proud of yourself?"

OOB reached out and took her arm and she yanked it from him.

"I want all of you outta here!" She yelled this, pointing at the group under Martyr Stand. "Especially you kids!" She pointed at her husband. "You play with guns and look what happens! Innocent people get convicted."

Cops led Spam and Reveered away.

Reveered's wife looked on from behind. "Henry? What have *you* done?"

A few cops made the crowd of teenagers hold still until one could enter the group and bag Reveered's paintball gun. Then they holstered their weapons. The dangerous part of fugitive arrest was over. They survived.

Two cops held Spam by each elbow and two others held Reveered and escorted the perps down Martyr Hill to the waiting cop cars in a sea of blue and red flashers.

Spam looked at the man in camo. "Henry, what have you done?"

"Hey Spam. Luke said you might come. I guess we're the one's who killed those boys," Reveered said. "Did you kill them?"

"No." Spam said.

"I suggest both of to stay quiet!" a cop said.

"Did you kill them?" Spam asked.

"No." Reveered said.

"Shut up. Both of you!"

"But shutting up is opposite of speaking into chaos," Reveered said to the cop.

"What do you do here?" Spam asked.

"Holy War."

"What's that?"

"It's where I teach innocent people how to handle injustice."

"You serious?" a cop asked.

A man took out a knife and cut the rope from Watson's wrist. Watson pulled the rag from his mouth, clutched the rope around his neck and threw up.

"You messed your clothes. You sure you're going to give the money back?"

"Yes sir!" Watson rasped. "Every penny! Then some!"

"See!" the man turned to his brothers. "He'll do right." He lifted the knife and cut the rope that pinned Watson's throat to the tree.

It was a good thing too.

The ground seemed to lift about three feet in a sudden jolt and they all fell as a sole flash of white fire shot upwards in a billow that reached over a thousand feet high. Sound fury steamed the air and toppled trees. A blizzard of leaves started flying around them and they fought for balance.

As they got their feet under them, the whistling started and they all dove for cover as debris and flying projectiles from the explosion started raining down pieces of barn across Thompson land as the blast radius extended itself outward to its full capacity.

28

Law Dogs

The faces of Spam and Reveered turned orange when the explosion cooled in the air and changed color. The fire ball ballooned into the night about a half mile to the north east. For a brief moment, daylight seemed to cover the area. Holy War soldiers screamed to high heaven and the cops stood and stared like dead men.

Then the cops formed three groups. One rushed the woods in the direction of the fire as if Napoleon himself was on his horse leading them. Others darted and dove into their cars like they do in bad hail storms and the third tier of agents decided to look before they reaped and went to their radios. Either which way it worked out, all the cops were soon chasing after the bigger fish to fry.

Mrs. Witherbean fell to her knees in awe then lunged up and ran into her house screaming something about Armageddon's Millstone and slammed and locked her doors to safeguard against the asteroid.

As the moment was thrust upon her, Angie Stone held her Bible high with both hands. "EPBS at my house! EPBS at my house!" She bellowed out. Soon all of AGA were outside their cars standing in the dust clouds from the cop cruisers that had just roared off, sirens blaring.

Regular Baptist Youth, with their former leader being carted off to jail, now looked at Angie. It was her time.

It then dawned on Angie that all of RBY was following her. "We go now to my house!" she pointed to town as she called out and climbed in her car. White knuckled she held the wheel and drove on. She looked down at her phone and decided not to warn her mother. The house might not be in top shape and that meant trouble for Angie. She wasn't sure how to run Emergency Prayer and Bible Study with her mom spouting off how the house hadn't been prepared for guest. Angie hunkered down behind the wheel. "Oh well," she said. "Hardship comes with leadership."

Mutt crammed Pamela under two large fallen trees. He clamped a hand over her mouth as she started to scream. Being between the blast and what appeared to be all of Tremble's cops only meant one thing. So he hid, and hid good.

Cops stormed by. Some splashed the creek below, others by land. They had their flashlights out and they were blazing a trail of light as they plowed through the underbrush.

The shock wave from the blast seemed to have upset the stillness of the forest. He then felt Pamela's hot breath on his hand from her hot lips. He enjoyed it for a moment, then took his hand off her mouth.

"You think the cops got Spam?" he asked, helping Pamela out of the water.

"No," she said. Her bedraggled, soaked cheerleading outfit sagged on her and water still glistened off her bare arms and legs from when they had crossed the creek and she fell. "Spam dropped off Ryan and the rest, but he won't surrender. He's a killer. He won't go out until he kills you!" She looked at Mutt and blinked cold out of her eyes. Her face glowed white in the chill. "Or dies trying!"

"Maybe you too," Mutt said. He believed in sharing his wealth.

"You know what I think?" she asked.

"What?"

"I think he's still around here. The cops were flashing

before he arrived. He's around here hiding like us. Let's sniff him out. We get him and we get our life." She lifted her hand and he took it and they re-started their hunt.

Luke of AGA didn't know what to do. He knew enough to skip EPBS at Angie's house. That was a gimme. He looked up at Reveered's place and moped that way. Reveered's wife was going to be a basket case and visiting her, because of her husband's arrest, was probably the right thing to do. He knew she was capable of blowing up a couple of more times because she was wound pretty tight. He expected her not to answer or if she did, to slam the door on him. But he was here, and he felt calming her down is what Jesus would do.

As he approached the steps, a boy with five girls came out of the darkness. It was Ryan. They had been at the tree for some reason and the girls had been wrapped in blankets like squaws, but in the chaos, nobody seemed to be able to figure out why.

"What's up, Ryan? What's with the harem?" Luke asked, then he stared at a bloody rag on Susan's face. "Ouch, Susan," he said to her.

"Spam brought us here," Ryan said.

"Why?" Luke asked.

"We followed him," a girl said. "And Susan's hurt."

Luke nodded. Then looked at a strip of clothe on her cheek. "You're still bleeding."

"You the one that invited Spam?" Ryan asked.

Luke nodded.

"Well, you got us instead."

The door flew open.

It was Reveered's wife. Her eyes flared. "I told you I wanted you *gone*! Now skedattle!" She screamed and slammed the door.

Luke turned back to the visitors. "Welcome to Holy War," he said and he went back up to the door and knocked again.

It opened slow and this time the woman looked at the girls and focused on the blankets and their exposure. Something clicked. "Your bleeding, Susan," she said.

"Help us," Ryan said.

The woman glared at Luke for some reason, then saw the refugees and waved them inside. "My husband put you up to this?"

Ryan shook his head. "Spam did. These ladies need your help."

Limping, gashed and chilled to the spine, they entered and Reveered's wife saw their exposure and just stared. "You just get off the Underground Railroad!" She looked out front. "Luke! Shut the door!"

Luke turned and saw a car come up Reveered's drive and stepped outside to watch it and closed the door behind him.

Deontra parked the car and shut off her engine. She got out. "Is this Reveered's house and AGA?"

He looked at the girl. "Hey Deontra."

"Yes."

"I'm Luke," he extended a handshake. "We met over Spam's teeth, remember? Today after lunch?"

"Where is everybody?"

"Our leader just got snagged by the cops and everyone scattered."

"Bummer. What for?"

"Murder."

"He didn't do it."

"I know. It was Spam. But the cops busted them both."

"Spam?" She looked at Luke with a confident doubt. "He didn't do it either. What do you do here? What's Holy War?"

"How did you hear about that?"

"Wendell's mom told me about it. She said he's here." She took a step towards the back yard because the fire was still burning up on the hill. "Did I miss him?"

Luke thought back, trying to recall if he had seen the blond kid who never talks around tonight. "I don't think he's here," he said, following after and staring at her long black hair. He felt inspired. "Holy War is where Reveered teaches us to face evil and get creamed."

"What kind of evil?" she stopped and looked at him.

"Well," Luke opened his palms. "Evil like bad laws that may come to America sometime in the future."

"So he teaches you to break these laws?"

"No. Not really. He teaches us how rather to oppose them and like, I don't know, go to jail or something."

"So he has a jail here? Like a Hide-an-Seek jail?"

Luke blushed at this. "No. We're beyond jail. We get executed for standing. Executed on Martyr Hill at Execution Tree." Saying that sounded cool.

"My parents are in jail right now too. Overnight at least. So's my priest and some nuns."

"Well, then you'll fit right in," Luke said.

She looked into his face then. She measured his eyes and his character. "He teaches you to know the purpose of suffering?"

"I guess. A soldier who knows his death is gain is marked by his Maker as a great display. It's who God wants us to be."

"Well said, Luke. I like that," she nodded approval. "Take me to this Martyr Hill."

She might have said more, but all Luke remembered is that she had rembered his name.

Wendell was alone in a tree on a hill at night. He felt like he was a dog in a storybook, Go Dog! Go!, and he was whirly in his thoughts. Dozens of cops had invaded the area below him! Arrest were handed out to innocent people for his crimes. And someone had just blown up what looked like a propane tank factory out in the forest and scattered all the cops.

And now all was quiet, so he started climbing down until he saw two people coming up the hill.

He froze because he could recognize Deontra's hair anywhere.

Deontra was walking up to Execution Stand on Martyr Hill.

He frowned and held still. *My mom told her. I suppose she'll tell me turn myself in and spend the rest of my life in prison.* His eyes followed out along the branch on which he stood and saw the knot that held rope. For some reason, he held himself against the dark shadow of the huge oak. His stomach did a flip and he thought back to the time he held her hand.

The same arrow now dug into his wrist. Not recognizing who was with her, he pulled out the arrow and held it in his hands.

"What's the rope for?" Deontra asked.

"We hold it and act like we're tied. Only we're not tied. We pretend we're tied so if we ever get tied we actually know we're free. Does that make sense?" Luke asked.

She shook her head.

What's that for?" Deontra pointed at the radio.

"We play a song, Jesus Freak, you know. Because that's why we're getting creamed. Because we're Jesus Freaks. Hopefully. Anyways."

"What's a Jesus Freak?"

"It's confusing. But it's basically a person who's intolerant of evil."

"Are you intolerant of evil?"

"Dunno. Sometimes, maybe."

"Hello Deontra!" Mutt said and walked up under the tree. "Good to see you." It was a low tone. A dark one. One that held bad hidden meanings.

Deontra stepped against Luke.

Luke felt her close and became nervous.

"Don't be nervous, Deontra." Pamela said, standing next to Mutt in her droopy cheer top and skirt.

Mutt came into Luke's personal space, circled and looked around. He picked up the radio boombox and looked at it.

Pamela looked around too. She walked to the other side of the tree and glanced around it. "Deontra, I think we're alone now. I do not think anyone else is around."

"Luke is here. So we're like, you know, not really alone."

"Why *were* all the cops here, Lukey Luke?" Mutt asked.

"Oh. Those guys," Luke said and waved them off as if dozens of law enforcement agents routinely came to AGA. "They made some arrest."

"Who?" Pamela asked.

"I think they're wrong for taking Reveered. He wouldn't kill anyone for real. He's the Devil's advocate. But not the killer. The other was Spam, you know, Spam from the Lunch Thing at school."

"So the cops came and took away the bad guys. Why didn't they take Mutt?" Pamela asked.

Luke shrugged, not knowing what to say.

"Oh that's right! He was hiding!" Pamela said.

Mutt lifted the stereo like a baseball bat and shattered it over Luke's head, collapsing the boy. "Boombox!" He said.

Deontra froze.

"Luke's not with you anymore!" Pamela said as Mutt

pushed Deontra over to the rope. "I told you he's bad!"

Mutt took up Deontra's hands and tied them behind her back with the rope hanging down from the tree. He yanked it tight, keeping her body off balanced, forcing her to lean forward.

"HELP!" she yelled but Mutt's hand clamped her mouth and forced her chin up.

"I told you to eat what we gave you. I told you I would come for you!"

"Why would Mutt attack you, Deontra?" Pamela asked. "Is it because I sent him?"

Mutt yanked his hand back as Deontra tried to bite it, then he recoiled and cracked his open palm against her cheek.

Wendell reached out his left hand and took a high branch for balance and then took another quiet step out along the thick branch. His right hand clenched the arrow.

"I told you not to tell anyone!" Mutt growled.

"He'll kill you!" Deontra looked up into their eyes. She whipped her head, throwing her hair out of her face. Blood drooled down her chin and some hair stuck to her mouth. "He'll kill you both!"

"Deontra! We're so sorry. Your little killer Spam is back in his can! You had a little peeper. We know all that. And now that your peeper's doing pee pee with the big boys!" Pamela said and came behind and nudged up against Deontra as if she were a man. "That means it's time for you to meet a real monster. One who is hungrier than a pack of dogs and likes good treats!"

Deontra kicked back and lost her balance. She screamed out as she fell because her body twisted her arms high as the rope to the branch above went tight. She fought to her balance and stood still, wincing in pain.

Wendell had now taken a few more steps out onto the

branch. He froze at hearing of a monster. *How do they know I'm here?*

Deontra stopped fighting the rope, got her legs under her and looked up at Mutt. "The killer isn't Spam, Sid. Nor is he some pastor who stimulates war about the Bible's Tomorrow Land. The killer almost got you at school today, Sid. When you were wired and called in that swarm of cops? They *did* rescue you. They *did* save your life!"

Mutt pulled back his arm to strike but froze.

"You felt him, didn't you?" Deontra met his eyes.

"Shut her up!" Pamela yelled!

Deontra's eyes were dark, but he saw the whites of her war eyes as she lifted her face to him. "You can hit me, hurt me and rape me, but I held his hand after they took you away crying and do you know what?"

Pamela rushed in and took Deontra by the hair and yanked her up against the will of her arms.

Deontra winced violently as her shoulders cried in pain.

Mutt took Pamela's hand and eased Deontra's pain.

"Too late, Mutt!" Deontra smiled sharply. "I held his hand! I forgave you and I forgive you now, but not him! He doesn't forgive you."

"Who killed my friends?" He reached out his hand and grabbed her by the neck and faced her.

"Along his arm was a black arrow! In his palm was the arrowhead. I'm more afraid of him than all of you! He's coming Mutt. The true killer comes. He'll kill all of you! He's the Death Angel of God Himself and he comes, Mutt. I'm so sorry but he comes for you all. I thought I could stop him. I thought he was a boy but he's not. I thought by forgiving you that I could change him. I thought he was human but he's not. That I could reason with him, but I can't. I talked to his parents but they don't know him. They don't know him like

I do and I'm so sorry for all of this. I brought all this death to you and he comes. He'll be bad Mutt. He'll torture you and you'll beg for death! And he will give it to you!"

"What of the monster?" Pamela asked. "Why won't your little angel fight that?" Pamela stood in front of the off-balanced girl and turned Deontra so she could face her. "I told the dogs to rape you because of Ron and do you know what the monster said?"

Deontra looked at the girl.

Pamela back-handed her and spun the girl around to face it.

Deontra looked into a face of fur, oil and whiskers. Of eyes behind a sunken deer hide face with drooped ears. She tried to scream but her lungs iced over as the arms of a creature extended and opened fingers of long, white claws.

The claws lunged at her and grabbed her, groped her, piercing clothes and skin.

The rope holding Deontra arms fell to the ground as the Deontra's weight was pressed upon by the beast. She hit the ground, rolled and looked up into the night at the three faces above her. She saw Mutt, Pamela and the face of the deer beast. Then she saw the fourth face and it made her scream. From deep inside her the terror burst out of her lungs, for IT came down from the black sky and she knew it's name was Death!

Pamela saw the rope fall and she looked up. What seemed a branch rushed at her and she lifted her arms.

Wendell, after slicing the rope with the razor-tipped arrow, leapt up, rising nearly straight up off the branch to gain force. Below, the ground rushed up at incredible speed. The arrow in both hands, was being brought down. Brought down hard.

He had three targets, he choose two. His knees crushed into the masked monster. He could see behind the mask and make out the shape of a man. But he knew better. He knew by how it grabbed Deontra, how it knew where to grab that it was a monster. Both his knees came down on the back of the man's skull.

Bones crushed and Wendell's knees collapsed the man's shoulders and back.

Then his arrow came down. Aiming to pierce the center of Bam Bam's skull, death missed.

Pamela, warned by Deontra's terror, yanked herself back and threw her arms up.

Wendell's stab broke through Pamela's defenses and drove the razor straight down along her face, opening a gash from her forehead, through the eyebrow and down her cheek before finishing its arc and coming to a stop in the girl's bicep.

Wendell then bounced off the man and rolled against Deontra and stood up between her and Mutt.

Mutt turned tail and ran.

Pamela, blood cascading, screamed herself blind.

A cop with a gun appeared and Wendell saw the open barrel aimed at his chest.

He raised his hands in defeat.

Then the gun motioned him over. "Move," the cop said as he came and kicked off the deer-hide mask, opening up Gene Thompson's face to the firelight. He took the man by the shoulders, but the head leaned wrong to the right. Deputy Weary yanked and sat Thompson up but the head then bent wrong to the left.

The teacher was a rag doll with a broken neck.

Pamela screamed.

"Dr. Carp!" the cop yelled, but no one came.

Wendell looked at Deontra. He sat her up and freed her hands.

Pamela thrashed on her back, blood matting her hair to

the earth. She screamed for help but no one came.

"Go get him, Wendell!" Deontra said, taking off her outer sweatshirt to stem the blood flow of Pamela. She got the girl's hands away, pressed the gaping wound closed as best she could and held her shirt against the wound with direct pressure.

"You're lucky, young lady!" the cop said. He was breathing hard as he opened Gene Thompson's airway by placing a hand behind the broken neck and pulling down the lower jaw. With a stick he fished out the man's tongue. A rasping sound came fourth from the teacher. "You're one of the few who saw this Freak-Reign-of-Wreckage without getting ruined. We got him now! Who was the hero?"

"He's no hero. He's The Death Angel of God."

29
Day of the Dog

Mutt ran north, and hard. But he forgot one thing. He lacked stamina to escape. Then it dawned on him. Why am I running from him? I know him. That kid's a wimp! At this he stopped and dropped his hands to his knees.

All was dark.

All was still.

His panting calmed and he started to hear the normal sounds of the forest. Leaves stirred and branches groaned adjusting to the change in temperature. Evening bugs had gone quiet and night bugs started their racket. Sirens were ahead and to the right. *Sacred Keg is blown. Woe!*

Mutt stood tall and turned south and listened. Footfalls were coming hard, but they didn't come at him direct. They were now off to his left and heading north. *The chaser has missed me! He's running blind!* Searing with the image of Pamela's face sliced open and his leader crushed, he pivoted and chased the sound. *Ye Ha! The wimp is dead!*

Branches like whips cut into Wendell's cheeks as he gained on the fleeing image ahead of him. It moved like a deer as it dodged trees and saplings and it didn't take long for Wendell to realize that Mutt was *leading* him.

Mutt was *playing* with him.

He stopped and the figure ahead of him stopped too. "Come on!" it whispered. "Mutt's coming!" It was the voice of an adult.

Wendell turned. Behind him the woods were crashing in sound. He looked ahead at the man motioning him to run. Run he did.

At the wall of twisted trees and weather-bleached, uprooted stumps, the tall man reached down and took the boy's hand and hoisted him up. They climbed.

"I got you now!" Mutt screamed out from the woods. "It's just you and me. And you're in my turf now!"

Wendell and the man crossed over the logs and tree stump barrier and came to a tall, chain-link fence.

"Shhhh!" he man hushed and they climbed up and over, but feet did grind metal on metal as they breached the fence and landed on the other side.

From the tree mound, Mutt looked down. "You're dead now, you fool! We got you now!" He started calling and yelling, making noise for all the area. Then he saw beyond the fence and saw the blond-haired boy get framed in the headlamps of an ATV. The quad then started and the boy in the lights ran off.

"Father!" Mutt called out. He jumped down and nearly vaulted the fence. *My dad's left the cave to help me!*

Far away a lone ear pricked. Then another. Then dozens. Then several hundred. Then the rest. They were running.

The engine sound. It called to them in the night.

Gaunt skin bent around their hardship jutting ribs. Fur stood on end. Noses protruded, searching for scent. That lovely scent that took away their stomach pain. Eyes peered forward as they flew over the bone littered land. Finally they saw the light. The dashing bouncing light from which the foolish meals chased. Soon. They charged on. Their jowls wet with saliva.

"Father! Run him down! Bring him down! He's the one!" Mutt yelled out as he chased the ATV man and the fleeing killer. After several hundred paces, Mutt nearly caught the machine. It didn't speed away from him. Then he saw two people on the quad.

The blond haired boy looked behind him as he clutched Dr. Carp.

"Don't look back!" Carp yelled. "You'll never forget if you do!"

Maybe that's why Wendell looked. Maybe that's why he had to look. Wendell no longer wanted to see Deontra get beaten. Abused by both gang and beast. By girl and boy and man. He wanted to see her stand. Stand and face her enemies with the help of others. Maybe her God *would* rescue her. Maybe her God wouldn't. Maybe the purpose of God is shrouded in mystery. Maybe her God provides rescue on a different grid.

But I rescued! I, Wendell Shyly, had rescued Deontra from the world of rapist! He thought this as he watched one, then a dozen fanged wild dogs leap onto Mutt and bring him down.

Mutt fought himself to his feet and threw them off. Then the one named Sid Mongrel, who preferred to be called Mutt, looked back at the direction of the fence. He ran.

It was too far.

They attacked.

A dog pack attacked as one organism.

Dozens at once.

Three took hold of Mutt's throat and clamped.

The body stopped.

There were no screams for help. Wendell heard only growls over the sound of the ATV as the red tail light glowed the eyes of the canines around their meal like embers of a medieval fire.

Then there were hundreds, a countless number as the grasses of the lands became alive with dogs. They buried the body as a plague of starved mice would flood a dead sheep.

Weary and the posse opened the door to the cave and beamed in their flashlights. A wave of rich, rain-forest thick air exhaled from the opening and a man in a leather recliner turned his head to them.

By his feet was a small heater and a blanket was over the farmer's legs. A worn John Deere cap was perched on his head.

They approached.

The man pulled white string on his chest and two small headphones popped out of his ears and fell to his shirt. He looked into the light. Music grooved Led from the mini phones. "Man! Chill down the lights, GT. I'm losing sinc with my tunes, man!"

Weary put down his gas can.

The others lowered theirs too.

Weary then took out a flare and torched it, soaking the man in the chair with firelight.

"Red flame, Man! Far out!" Peter Mongrel said.

"Stone age is over, Mongrel. The Dog Days are done!" Weary said. He nodded and gas cans were kicked over.

A wave of dogs turned into the ATV like a line of attacking Zeros would a battleship. Wendell felt the driver tense as he worked the gears. Now the faster dogs, the alphas, came close. They were the ones who could run down live deer and lead the packs. They were aside Wendell, barking and biting out. They lunged at the tires and snapped for the flesh of his legs.

"Hang on boy!" Dr. Carp yelled and Wendell ducked

behind the man as a barn loomed. Carp looked back and yelled out in fear and awe.

The pack followed close. It had them.

The barn came at them and the machine smashed through the door, pressing both riders off the vehicle and sending them sprawling.

Then the dogs came. The big ones with their throats and chest wet with hunger.

Carp was on his feet and running to a barn beam that had ladder rungs attached to it. Shaking his legs free, he kicked hard, only to see that it was a boy grabbing on in desperation.

Teeth sinking deep through denim and flesh, Wendell screamed out as Carp lifted the boy to safety and shook off the last of the biting beast below.

They ascended and Carp pushed up a ceiling hatch and black sky appeared. "Up and out," he said. "Don't fall."

Wendell nodded. Sound advice. Simple to remember.

"Don't look down," Carp said.

The boy did. Hundreds of pairs of eyes caught the moonlight and beamed carnivore back up. Wendell shivered and slithered out onto the roof. He reached down and helped the man up.

Panting, Carp reached the roof and sat next to the boy. He slammed the hatch back down. "Name's Carp. John Carp!" He said.

"I'm Wendell."

"Nice to meet you."

"You're really Dr. Carp the animal killer?"

"Do those animals all look dead to you?"

Wendell breathed hard. Pain on his shoulder started calling about and blood ran warm down his leg and soaked his shoe. "I'm bit," he said.

"They do that."

"Why did you help me?" Wendell asked.

"Nice view from here!" Carp pointed east to Thompson land. Smoldering trees were sending grey smoke against the night sky and patches of orange flames flickered near the flashing red and blue strobes.

"Do you know who I am?" Wendell asked.

"Sorta."

"Do you know what I've down?"

"Pretty much."

"Gene Thompson said that you were kicked out of the Army," Wendell said.

"Yup."

"How come?"

"Murder."

"Is that why you save the lives of these dogs?"

"I try to save all life."

"Can you?"

"Sometimes."

"Does that help?"

"It helps me."

"Did they need to be killed? The soldiers?"

"I like you Wendell."

"Did they?"

"No. The one's I killed were suffering bad. Burned something awful. Maimed. Disfigured and incapacitated, delimbed and defenseless, but they were people, Wendell."

"Wow."

"They were human beings like Mutt back there," Carp thumbed the direction of the feeding frenzy.

Both now looked out across the night. Patches of ground became visible here and there and the horde drifted away from the barn back to their dens. Sirens in the west by Reveered's seemed to have stopped altogether but new one's now sounded off in the woods at the big bowl in the ground where Sacred Keg used to be.

"Those are ambulances now coming to Holy War," Wendell said. "My mom's going to be really mad at me," the boy turned and looked at the man. "Did I do right?"

"I take it you're the killer?"

"Yup."

"Nope." Carp looked to the east. "Killing for revenge, protection, justice and self-defense is war. And war is the human heart at its very worse."

Wendell brought a thumb up to his mouth and bit the nail. "Oops," he said.

"Maybe you'll be okay," Carp said. "There is a greater evil than that of war."

"Good. Well, not good I guess. What is it?"

"The evil of injustice. Good has to kill those who do injustice."

"Well, that stinks. If we do nothing were screwed and if we do something were screwed too."

"Probably."

Wendell adjusted his sitting position and pulled out a loose nail from the roof and spun it out into the darkness. "You raised Spam?"

"Some."

"You talk like this a lot?"

"Some."

"Then he's lucky. Despite what happened to his parents and brother."

Carp took a shingle from the roof and slung it far off into the night. It made no sound as it landed.

"I shot an arrow once that sounded like that," Wendell said. A tear of hardship formed and ran along his cheek. "You think I done right, Carp?"

"Do you know what happened to Spam's mom?"
"She killed herself. Suicide."
"That she did. She also got herself raped by Gene Thompson back when she was a kid. Back when she was your age. It happened at Sacred Keg. She told her brother about it. That was him you met who was trying to put Humpty Dumpty back together. Thompson wasn't but five, maybe six years older than her at the time. Just a young teacher with some bad, bad issues."
"Really?"
"Really. Not a nice thought knowing that the pretty girl they had tied up under the tree might have someday killed herself after wrecking out her family."
"Deontra will be okay. She'll be okay."
"Good."
"She forgave them," Shyly said. "You know that? While they were going for her, she forgave them."
"And you? You forgive them? You forgive Thompson for what he did to Spam's ma? Deontra? How about the string of victims over his thirty-year terror?"
Wendell was silent.
"Hard questions Wendell. Hard questions. You ready for another one?"
"It can't get worse."
"Yes it can."
"How?"
"You rescued Deontra from Thompson."
"I did."
"And you rescued her from that screwed up, cheerleader, Bam Bam?"
"I did. She's the worst. She started it all. I cut her face bad, but..."
"You cut her face, huh?"

Day of the Dog

Wendell nodded.

"So you had a chance to rescue her from Gene the Monster. The beast that's been raping her since whenever. But instead you just sliced her face off? Why didn't you rescue her too since you were already in the rescue business?"

It went quiet then. The stillness came where one can hear the wings of bats, a lone moan of treed cat and the scrape of the moon across the dark sky.

Then Wendell stirred as if he was losing balance because of the earth turning on axis. "I don't want you to ask me anymore questions," he said as he thought about how he had opened up Pamela's face. "A lifetime in prison will go too quick for what I've done to her."

Carp nodded. He didn't want to ask anymore questions either. He had never wanted to ask. Never wanted to make the pain of anyone else be his business. But of late, he tried to never let what he wanted to do, interfere with what he did.

Wendell stood and looked way down at the ground and a few circling dogs.

"Thinking about jumping?" Carp asked.

"I told you not to ask me anymore questions."

"That you did, Wendell. That you did. But if you think about it. You're on a barn in the middle of 700 acres surrounded by a thousand starved dogs."

"So?"

"So why don't you just serve out your prison sentence here?"

Wendell turned from the man and looked down at the dogs.

Dozens were now looking up at him, but none wagged their tails.

The End

www.ingramcontent.com/pod-product-compliance
Lightning Source LLC
Chambersburg PA
CBHW061426040426
42450CB00007B/926